FLEXITARIAN

PLANT-BASED RECIPES WITH & WITHOUT THE MEAT

Publications International, Ltd.

Microwave Cooking: Microwave ovens vary in wattage. Use the cooking times as guidelines and check for doneness before adding more time.

WARNING: Food preparation, baking and cooking involve inherent dangers: misuse of electric products, sharp electric tools, boiling water, hot stoves, allergic reactions, foodborne illnesses and the like, pose numerous potential risks. Publications International, Ltd. (PIL) assumes no responsibility or liability for any damages you may experience as a result of following recipes, instructions, tips or advice in this publication.

While we hope this publication helps you find new ways to eat delicious foods, you may not always achieve the results desired due to variations in ingredients, cooking temperatures, typos, errors, omissions, or individual cooking abilities.

Let's get social!
 @Publications_International
 @PublicationsInternational
www.pilbooks.com

CONTENTS

BREAKFAST

CRUSTLESS SPINACH QUICHE

MAKES 6 SERVINGS

8 eggs

1 cup half-and-half

1 teaspoon Italian
   seasoning

¾ teaspoon salt

½ teaspoon black
   pepper

1 package (10 ounces)
   frozen chopped
   spinach, thawed
   and squeezed dry

1¼ cups (5 ounces)
    shredded Italian
    cheese blend

1. Preheat oven to 350°F. Spray 8-inch round cake pan with nonstick cooking spray.

2. Beat eggs, half-and-half, Italian seasoning, salt and pepper in medium bowl until well blended. Stir in spinach and cheese; mix well. Pour into prepared pan.

3. Bake 33 minutes or until toothpick inserted into center comes out clean. Remove to wire rack; cool 10 minutes before serving.

TIP

To remove quiche from pan for serving, run knife around edge of pan to loosen. Invert quiche onto plate; invert again onto second plate. Cut into wedges to serve.

QUINOA AND OAT MUESLI

MAKES 6¾ CUPS (ABOUT 12 SERVINGS)

- 1 cup uncooked quinoa
- 3 cups old-fashioned rolled oats
- ¼ cup unsweetened flaked coconut
- ¾ cup coarsely chopped almonds
- ½ teaspoon ground cinnamon
- ½ cup toasted wheat germ
- ¼ cup ground flaxseeds
- 1¼ cups dried fruit

1. Preheat oven to 350°F. Spread quinoa in single layer on baking sheet. Bake 8 to 10 minutes until toasted and golden brown, stirring frequently. (Quinoa will make a slight popping sound when almost done.) Remove to large bowl; cool completely.

2. Combine oats, coconut, almonds and cinnamon on same baking sheet; mix well. Spread in even layer. Bake 15 minutes or until mixture is toasted and fragrant but not burnt. Let cool completely.

3. Add oat mixture to cooled quinoa in large bowl with wheat germ, flaxseeds and dried fruit. Stir to combine.

ZUCCHINI-TOMATO FRITTATA

MAKES 4 SERVINGS

1 tablespoon olive oil

1 cup sliced zucchini

1 cup broccoli florets

1 cup diced red or
    yellow bell pepper

6 eggs

½ cup cottage cheese

½ cup rehydrated*
    sun-dried tomatoes
    (1 ounce dry),
    coarsely chopped

¼ cup chopped
    green onions

¼ cup chopped
    fresh basil

¾ teaspoon salt

⅛ teaspoon ground
    red pepper

2 tablespoons grated
    Parmesan cheese

*To rehydrate sun-dried
tomatoes, pour 1 cup
boiling water over tomatoes
in small bowl. Let stand 5 to
10 minutes or until softened;
drain well.*

1. Preheat broiler. Heat oil in large ovenproof nonstick skillet over medium-high heat. Add zucchini, broccoli and bell pepper; cook and stir 3 to 4 minutes or until vegetables are crisp-tender.

2. Beat eggs, cottage cheese, tomatoes, green onions, basil, salt and ground red pepper in medium bowl until well blended. Pour egg mixture over vegetables in skillet. Cook 7 to 8 minutes or until frittata is almost firm and golden brown on bottom, gently lifting edges of frittata to allow uncooked portion to flow underneath. Remove from heat; sprinkle with Parmesan.

3. Broil about 5 inches from heat 3 to 5 minutes or until top is golden brown. Cut into wedges.

EXTRA GREEN AVOCADO TOAST

MAKES 2 SERVINGS

- ½ **cup thawed frozen peas**
- 2 **teaspoons lemon juice**
- 1 **teaspoon minced fresh tarragon**
- ¼ **teaspoon plus ⅛ teaspoon salt, divided**
- ⅛ **teaspoon black pepper**
- 1 **teaspoon olive oil**
- 1 **tablespoon pepitas (raw pumpkin seeds)**
- 4 **slices hearty whole grain bread, toasted**
- 1 **avocado**

1. Combine peas, lemon juice, tarragon, ¼ teaspoon salt and pepper in small food processor; pulse until blended but still chunky. (Or combine all ingredients in small bowl and mash with fork to desired consistency.)

2. Heat oil in small saucepan over medium heat. Add pepitas; cook and stir 1 to 2 minutes or until toasted. Transfer to small bowl; stir in remaining ⅛ teaspoon salt.

3. Spread about 1 tablespoon pea mixture over each slice of bread. (Store any remaining pea mixture in airtight container in refrigerator for a day or two.)

4. Cut avocado in half lengthwise around pit. If making one serving, wrap one half with pit in plastic wrap and store in refrigerator for 1 day. Cut avocado into slices in the shell; use spoon to scoop out slices. Arrange avocado slices over pea mixture; top with toasted pepitas.

FETA BRUNCH BAKE

MAKES 4 SERVINGS

1	medium red bell pepper
2	packages (10 ounces each) fresh spinach, stemmed
6	eggs
1½	cups (6 ounces) crumbled feta cheese
⅓	cup chopped onion
2	tablespoons chopped fresh parsley
¼	teaspoon dried dill weed
	Dash black pepper

1. Preheat broiler. Place bell pepper on foil-lined broiler pan. Broil 4 inches from heat source 15 to 20 minutes or until blackened on all sides, turning with tongs every 5 minutes. Place in paper bag; close bag and set aside to cool 15 to 20 minutes. Remove core; cut bell pepper in half and rub off skin. Rinse under cold water. Cut into ½-inch pieces.*

2. Fill medium saucepan half full with water; bring to a boil over high heat. Add spinach; return to a boil. Boil 2 to 3 minutes or until wilted. Drain spinach; immediately plunge into bowl of cold water. Drain and let stand until cool enough to handle. Squeeze spinach to remove excess water; finely chop.

3. Preheat oven to 400°F. Spray 1-quart baking dish with nonstick cooking spray.

4. Beat eggs in large bowl until foamy. Stir in roasted pepper, spinach, cheese, onion, parsley, dill weed and black pepper. Pour into prepared baking dish.

5. Bake 20 minutes or until set. Let stand 5 minutes before serving.

Or use 1 jarred roasted pepper, cut into ½-inch pieces. Proceed to step 2.

SLOW-COOKED SHAKSHUKA

MAKES 6 SERVINGS

¼ cup extra virgin olive oil

1 medium onion, chopped

1 large red bell pepper, chopped

3 cloves garlic, sliced

1 can (28 ounces) crushed tomatoes with basil, garlic and oregano

2 teaspoons paprika

2 teaspoons ground cumin

2 teaspoons sugar

½ teaspoon salt

¼ teaspoon red pepper flakes

¾ cup crumbled feta cheese

6 eggs

SLOW COOKER DIRECTIONS

1. Combine oil, onion, bell pepper, garlic, tomatoes, paprika, cumin, sugar, salt and red pepper flakes in slow cooker; mix well.

2. Cover; cook on HIGH 3 hours. Stir in cheese. Break eggs, one at a time, onto top of tomato mixture, leaving small amount of space between each.

3. Cover; cook on HIGH 15 to 18 minutes or until the egg whites are set but yolks are still creamy. Scoop eggs and sauce into serving bowls or plates.

VEGETABLE QUINOA FRITTATA

MAKES 6 SERVINGS

1 tablespoon olive oil

1 cup diced onion

1 cup small broccoli florets

¾ cup finely chopped red bell pepper

2 cloves garlic, minced

1¼ teaspoons kosher salt

Black pepper

1½ cups cooked quinoa

¼ cup sun-dried tomatoes, chopped

8 eggs, lightly beaten

¼ cup grated Parmesan cheese

1. Preheat oven to 400°F.

2. Heat oil in large ovenproof nonstick skillet over medium-high heat. Add onion and broccoli; cook and stir 4 minutes. Add bell pepper; cook and stir 2 minutes. Add garlic, salt and black pepper; cook and stir 30 seconds. Stir in quinoa and sun-dried tomatoes.

3. Gently stir in eggs; cook until softly scrambled. Sprinkle with cheese.

4. Bake about 7 minutes or until eggs are set. Let stand 5 minutes before cutting into wedges.

BAKED PUMPKIN OATMEAL

MAKES 6 SERVINGS

- 2 cups old-fashioned oats
- 2 cups milk
- 1 cup canned pumpkin
- 2 eggs
- ⅓ cup packed brown sugar
- 1 teaspoon vanilla
- ½ cup dried cranberries, plus additional for topping
- 1 teaspoon pumpkin pie spice
- ½ teaspoon salt
- ½ teaspoon baking powder
- Maple syrup
- Chopped pecans (optional)

1. Preheat oven to 350°F. Spray 8-inch square baking dish with nonstick cooking spray.

2. Spread oats on ungreased baking sheet. Bake 10 minutes or until fragrant and lightly browned, stirring occasionally. Pour into medium bowl; let cool slightly.

3. Whisk milk, pumpkin, eggs, brown sugar and vanilla in large bowl until well blended. Add ½ cup cranberries, pumpkin pie spice, salt and baking powder to oats; mix well. Add oat mixture to pumpkin mixture; stir until well blended. Pour into prepared baking dish.

4. Bake 45 minutes or until set and knife inserted into center comes out almost clean. Serve warm with maple syrup, additional cranberries and pecans, if desired.

GREEK ISLES OMELET

MAKES 2 SERVINGS

1 tablespoon olive oil, divided

¼ cup chopped onion

¼ cup canned artichoke hearts, rinsed and drained

¼ cup chopped fresh spinach

¼ cup chopped plum tomato

2 tablespoons sliced pitted black olives, rinsed and drained

4 eggs

½ teaspoon salt

Dash black pepper

1. Heat half of oil in small nonstick skillet over medium heat. Add onion; cook and stir 2 minutes or until crisp-tender. Add artichokes; cook and stir until heated through. Stir in spinach, tomato and olives; cook 1 minute. Remove to small bowl.

2. Wipe out skillet with paper towels. Beat eggs, salt and pepper in medium bowl until well blended.

3. Heat remaining oil in skillet over medium heat. Pour egg mixture into skillet; cook and stir gently, lifting edges of omelet to allow uncooked portion to flow underneath. Cook just until set.

4. Spoon vegetable mixture over half of omelet; gently loosen omelet with spatula and fold in half. Serve immediately.

QUINOA BREAKFAST "FRIED RICE"

MAKES 4 SERVINGS

- 1 **cup uncooked quinoa**
- 1½ **cups water**
- ¼ **teaspoon kosher salt, divided**
- 2 **tablespoons grapeseed or avocado oil, divided**
- 1 **carrot, finely diced**
- ¾ **cup frozen peas**
- 4 **ounces ham, finely diced (optional)**
- 2 **green onions, thinly sliced**
- 2 **teaspoons minced garlic**
- 1 **teaspoon grated ginger**
- 3 **eggs, lightly beaten**
- 1 **tablespoon reduced-sodium soy sauce, plus additional for serving**
- 1 **tablespoon ketchup**
- ¼ **teaspoon black pepper**

1. Place quinoa in fine-mesh strainer; rinse well under cold water. Combine quinoa, 1½ cups water and ⅛ teaspoon salt in large saucepan; bring to a boil over medium-high heat. Reduce heat to low; cover and cook about 15 minutes or until quinoa is tender and water is absorbed. Spread on baking sheet; cool completely.

2. Heat 1 tablespoon oil in large nonstick skillet over medium-high heat. Add carrot and peas; cook and stir 4 minutes or until softened. Add ham, if desired; cook about 2 minutes or until lightly browned. Add green onions, garlic and ginger; cook about 1 minute or until fragrant. Transfer to large bowl.

3. Heat remaining 1 tablespoon oil in skillet over medium-high heat. Add eggs and remaining ⅛ teaspoon salt; cook about 1 minute or until lightly scrambled and set. Break up eggs into small, bite-size pieces with spatula.

4. Return carrot-pea mixture to skillet. Add quinoa; cook and stir 2 minutes. Add 1 tablespoon soy sauce, ketchup and pepper; cook and stir 1 minute or until heated through. Serve with additional soy sauce, if desired.

TIP

Prepare the quinoa the night before and refrigerate, then begin with step 2 when you're ready to cook the next day.

EDAMAME FRITTATA

MAKES 4 SERVINGS

- **2 tablespoons olive oil**
- **½ cup frozen shelled edamame**
- **⅓ cup frozen corn**
- **¼ cup chopped shallot**
- **6 eggs**
- **¾ teaspoon Italian seasoning**
- **½ teaspoon salt**
- **½ teaspoon black pepper**
- **¼ cup chopped green onions**
- **½ cup crumbled goat cheese**

1. Preheat broiler. Heat oil in large ovenproof nonstick skillet over medium-high heat. Add edamame, corn and shallot; cook and stir 6 to 8 minutes or until shallot is lightly browned.

2. Meanwhile, beat eggs, Italian seasoning, salt and pepper in medium bowl. Stir in green onions.

3. Pour egg mixture over vegetables in skillet; sprinkle with cheese. Cook over medium heat 5 to 7 minutes or until eggs are set on bottom, gently lifting edges of frittata to allow uncooked portion to flow underneath.

4. Broil 6 inches from heat 1 minute or until top is puffy and golden brown. Loosen frittata from skillet with spatula; slide onto small platter. Cut into wedges.

SALADS

GREEK SALAD

MAKES 6 SERVINGS

SALAD

- 3 medium tomatoes, cut into 8 wedges each and seeds removed
- 1 green bell pepper, cut into 1-inch pieces
- ½ English cucumber (8 to 10 inches), quartered lengthwise and sliced crosswise
- ½ red onion, thinly sliced
- ½ cup pitted kalamata olives
- 8 ounces feta cheese, cut into ½-inch cubes

DRESSING

- 6 tablespoons extra virgin olive oil
- 3 tablespoons red wine vinegar
- 1 to 2 cloves garlic, minced
- ¾ teaspoon dried oregano
- ¾ teaspoon salt
- ¼ teaspoon black pepper

1. For salad, combine tomatoes, bell pepper, cucumber, onion and olives in large bowl. Top with cheese.

2. For dressing, whisk oil, vinegar, garlic, oregano, salt and black pepper in medium bowl until well blended.

3. Pour dressing over salad; toss gently to coat.

ASPARAGUS AND ARUGULA SALAD

MAKES 4 TO 6 SERVINGS

½ cup sun-dried tomatoes (not packed in oil)

1 cup boiling water

1 cup sliced asparagus (1-inch pieces)

1 package (5 ounces) baby arugula

½ cup shaved Parmesan cheese

¼ cup extra virgin olive oil

2 tablespoons lemon juice

1 tablespoon orange juice

1 clove garlic, minced

½ teaspoon salt

½ teaspoon grated lemon peel

⅛ teaspoon black pepper

1. Place sun-dried tomatoes in small bowl; pour 1 cup boiling water over tomatoes. Let stand 5 minutes; drain well.

2. Bring medium saucepan of salted water to a boil. Add asparagus; cook 1 minute or until crisp-tender. Rinse under cold running water to stop cooking.

3. Combine arugula, asparagus, sun-dried tomatoes and cheese in large bowl. Whisk oil, lemon juice, orange juice, garlic, salt, lemon peel and pepper in small bowl until well blended. Pour dressing over salad; toss gently to coat.

STRAWBERRY POPPY SEED CHICKEN SALAD

MAKES 4 SERVINGS

DRESSING

- ¼ cup white wine vinegar
- 2 tablespoons orange juice
- 2 teaspoons honey
- 2 teaspoons poppy seeds
- 1½ teaspoons Dijon mustard
- ½ teaspoon salt
- ½ teaspoon minced dried onion
- ½ cup avocado or grapeseed oil

SALAD

- 8 cups romaine lettuce
- 2 cups grilled or roasted chicken breast strips
- ¾ cup fresh pineapple chunks
- ¾ cup sliced fresh strawberries
- ¾ cup fresh blueberries
- 1 navel orange, peeled and sectioned
- ¼ cup chopped toasted pecans*

  To toast pecans, cook in small skillet over medium heat until lightly browned, stirring frequently.

1. For dressing, whisk vinegar, orange juice, honey, poppy seeds, mustard, salt and dried onion in small bowl until well blended. Slowly add oil, whisking until well blended.

2. For salad, combine romaine and two thirds of dressing in large bowl; toss gently to coat.

3. Divide salad among four plates, top with chicken, pineapple, strawberries, blueberries, oranges and pecans. Serve with remaining dressing.

SHRIMP AND SOBA NOODLE SALAD

MAKES 4 SERVINGS

- 6 ounces soba noodles
- 1 tablespoon vegetable oil
- 2 cups diagonally sliced green beans (bite-size pieces)
- 1½ cups sliced mushrooms
- 1½ cups (6 ounces) medium cooked shrimp (with tails on)
- ½ cup thinly sliced red bell pepper
- 2 tablespoons orange juice
- 2 tablespoons lime juice
- 1 tablespoon soy sauce
- 2 teaspoons dark sesame oil
- 2 tablespoons finely chopped fresh cilantro
- 1 to 2 tablespoons toasted sesame seeds (optional)

1. Cook noodles according to package directions; drain and rinse under warm water. Drain again; transfer to large bowl.

2. Heat vegetable oil in large skillet over medium-high heat. Add green beans and mushrooms; cook 8 minutes or until mushrooms are lightly browned and beans are softened, stirring occasionally. Add to bowl with noodles. Stir in shrimp and bell pepper.

3. Whisk orange juice, lime juice, soy sauce and sesame oil in small bowl until well blended. Pour over salad; toss gently to coat. Sprinkle with cilantro and sesame seeds, if desired.

SWEET AND SAVORY SWEET POTATO SALAD

MAKES 6 SERVINGS

4   cups peeled chopped cooked sweet potatoes (4 to 6)

¾   cup chopped green onions

½   cup chopped fresh parsley

½   cup dried unsweetened cherries

¼   cup plus 2 tablespoons rice wine vinegar

2   tablespoons extra virgin olive oil

2   tablespoons coarse ground mustard

¾   teaspoon garlic powder

½   teaspoon salt

¼   teaspoon black pepper

1. Combine sweet potatoes, green onions, parsley and cherries in large bowl.

2. Whisk vinegar, oil, mustard, garlic powder, salt and pepper in small bowl until well blended.

3. Pour dressing over sweet potato mixture; toss gently to coat. Serve immediately or cover and refrigerate until ready to serve.

TOMATO WATERMELON SALAD

MAKES 4 SERVINGS

¼ **cup extra virgin olive oil**

2 **tablespoons fresh lemon juice**

½ **teaspoon honey**

½ **teaspoon salt**

⅛ **teaspoon black pepper**

2 **large heirloom tomatoes (about 10 ounces each), cut into 6 slices each**

2 **cups cubed watermelon (about 12 ounces)**

¼ **cup thinly sliced red onion rings**

¼ **cup crumbled feta cheese**

Fresh chervil or parsley sprigs (optional)

1. Whisk oil, lemon juice, honey, salt and pepper in small bowl until well blended.

2. Arrange tomato slices on four salad plates. Top with watermelon and onion rings; sprinkle with cheese.

3. Drizzle dressing over salad; garnish with chervil.

SUPERFOOD KALE SALAD

MAKES 4 SERVINGS

MAPLE-ROASTED CARROTS

- **8** carrots, trimmed
- **2** tablespoons maple syrup
- **2** tablespoons olive oil
- **½** teaspoon salt
- **⅛** teaspoon black pepper
- Dash ground red pepper

MAPLE-LEMON VINAIGRETTE

- **¼** cup extra virgin olive oil
- **2** tablespoons maple syrup
- **3** tablespoons lemon juice
- **¾** teaspoon grated lemon peel
- **½** teaspoon salt
- **⅛** teaspoon black pepper

SALAD

- **4** cups chopped kale
- **2** cups mixed greens
- **1** cup dried cranberries
- **1** cup slivered almonds, toasted
- **1** cup shredded Parmesan cheese

1. Preheat oven to 400°F. Line baking sheet with parchment paper. Spray 13×9-inch baking pan with nonstick cooking spray.

2. Place carrots on prepared baking sheet. Whisk 2 tablespoons maple syrup, 2 tablespoons oil, ½ teaspoon salt, ⅛ teaspoon black pepper and red pepper in small bowl until well blended. Brush some of oil mixture over carrots. Roast 30 minutes or until carrots are tender, brushing with oil mixture and shaking pan every 10 minutes. Cut carrots crosswise into ¼-inch slices when cool enough to handle.

3. While carrots are roasting, prepare vinaigrette. Whisk ¼ cup oil, 2 tablespoons maple syrup, lemon juice, lemon peel, ½ teaspoon salt and ⅛ teaspoon black pepper in small bowl until well blended.

4. Combine kale, greens, cranberries, almonds and cheese in large bowl. Add carrots. Pour vinaigrette over salad; toss to coat.

PESTO FARRO SALAD WITH PEAS, ASPARAGUS AND FETA

MAKES 4 SERVINGS

- **1 cup uncooked pearled farro**
- **1 cup peas**
- **1 bunch asparagus, trimmed and cut into 1-inch pieces**
- **2 cups fresh packed basil leaves**
- **½ cup packed fresh Italian parsley**
- **¼ cup toasted walnuts***
- **2 cloves garlic**
- **½ cup extra virgin olive oil**
- **½ cup grated Parmesan cheese**
- **Kosher salt and black pepper**
- **½ cup crumbled feta cheese**

*To toast walnuts, cook in small skillet over medium heat 2 to 3 minutes or until lightly browned, stirring frequently.

1. Bring large saucepan of water to a boil over high heat. Add farro; reduce heat to medium-low. Cook about 30 minutes or until tender, adding peas during last 5 minutes of cooking time and asparagus during last 2 minutes of cooking time. Drain well.

2. Meanwhile, combine basil, parsley, walnuts and garlic in food processor; pulse until coarsely chopped. With motor running, add oil in thin, steady stream. Add Parmesan; pulse to combine. Season with salt and pepper.

3. Transfer farro mixture to large bowl. Add ¾ cup pesto mixture; toss to coat. (Reserve remaining pesto for another use.) Add feta; stir gently to combine. Season with additional salt and pepper, if desired.

FARMERS' MARKET POTATO SALAD

MAKES 6 SERVINGS

Pickled Red Onions
(recipe follows)

2 cups cubed assorted
potatoes (purple,
baby red, Yukon
Gold and/or a
combination)

1 cup fresh green
beans, cut into
1-inch pieces

2 tablespoons plain
Greek yogurt

2 tablespoons white
wine vinegar

2 tablespoons olive oil

1 tablespoon spicy
mustard

1 teaspoon salt

1. Prepare Pickled Red Onions.

2. Bring large saucepan of water to a boil.
Add potatoes; cook 5 to 8 minutes or until
fork-tender.* Add green beans during last
4 minutes of cooking time. Drain potatoes
and green beans.

3. Whisk yogurt, vinegar, oil, mustard and salt
in large bowl until smooth and well blended.

4. Add potatoes, green beans and Pickled
Red Onions to dressing; toss gently to coat.
Cover and refrigerate at least 1 hour before
serving to allow flavors to develop.

*Some potatoes take longer to cook than others.
Remove potatoes to medium bowl with slotted
spoon when fork-tender.*

PICKLED RED ONIONS

MAKES ABOUT ½ CUP

½ cup thinly sliced
red onion

¼ cup white wine
vinegar

2 tablespoons water

1 teaspoon sugar

½ teaspoon salt

Combine all ingredients in large glass jar;
seal jar and shake well. Refrigerate at least
1 hour or up to 1 week.

CAULIFLOWER CAPRESE SALAD

MAKES 8 SERVINGS

- 1 head cauliflower, cut into florets and thinly sliced
- ¾ cup balsamic vinegar
- ½ cup olive oil
- 1 teaspoon salt
- 1 teaspoon sugar
- 1 clove garlic, minced
- 1 teaspoon Italian seasoning
- 1 container (8 ounces) pearl-shaped fresh mozzarella cheese *or* 1 (8-ounce) ball fresh mozzarella, chopped
- 2 cups chopped fresh tomatoes *or* 1 pint grape tomatoes, halved
- ¼ cup shredded fresh basil

1. Place cauliflower in large resealable food storage bag or large bowl. Add vinegar, oil, salt, sugar, garlic and Italian seasoning; seal bag and shake to coat. Marinate in refrigerator 8 hours or overnight.

2. Pour cauliflower and marinade into large bowl. Add cheese, tomatoes and basil; stir gently to coat.

TIPS

Turn leftovers into a great entrée. Cook pasta (any shape) according to package directions. Drain and immediately toss with leftover caprese salad. You can bulk up the leftovers even more by adding protein: Gently stir in chopped cooked chicken or fish with the pasta, or for a vegetarian version, stir in a can of drained and rinsed cannellini beans. Serve warm or at room temperature.

KOHLRABI AND CARROT SLAW

MAKES 8 SERVINGS

2 pounds kohlrabi bulbs, peeled and shredded

2 medium carrots, shredded

1 small red bell pepper, chopped

8 cherry tomatoes, halved

2 green onions, thinly sliced

¼ cup mayonnaise

¼ cup plain yogurt

2 tablespoons cider vinegar

2 tablespoons finely chopped fresh parsley

1 teaspoon dried dill weed

½ teaspoon salt

¼ teaspoon ground cumin

⅛ teaspoon black pepper

1. Combine kohlrabi, carrots, bell pepper, tomatoes and green onions in medium bowl.

2. Whisk mayonnaise, yogurt, vinegar, parsley, dill weed, salt, cumin and black pepper in small bowl until well blended.

3. Add dressing to vegetables; toss to coat. Cover and refrigerate until ready to serve.

QUINOA TABBOULEH

MAKES 6 TO 8 SERVINGS

- 1 cup uncooked tricolor quinoa *or* ½ cup *each* red and white quinoa
- 2 cups water
- 2 teaspoons salt, divided
- 2 cups chopped fresh tomatoes (red, orange or a combination)
- 1 cucumber, quartered lengthwise and thinly sliced
- ¼ cup extra virgin olive oil
- 3 tablespoons lemon juice
- ½ teaspoon black pepper
- 1 red or orange bell pepper, chopped
- ½ cup minced fresh parsley

1. Rinse quinoa in fine-mesh strainer under cold water. Combine 2 cups water, quinoa and 1 teaspoon salt in medium saucepan; bring to a boil over high heat. Reduce heat to low; cover and simmer 10 to 15 minutes until quinoa is tender and water is absorbed. Transfer to large bowl; cool to room temperature.

2. Meanwhile, combine tomatoes, cucumber and remaining 1 teaspoon salt in medium bowl. Let stand 20 minutes.

3. Stir tomatoes, cucumber and any accumulated juices into quinoa.

4. Whisk oil, lemon juice and black pepper in small bowl until well blended. Add to quinoa mixture with bell pepper and parsley; mix well. Taste and season with additional salt and pepper, if desired.

TIP

For a heartier dish, add a can of chickpeas, drained and rinsed, or a can of tuna, drained and flaked. Stir into the quinoa with the bell pepper.

CHARRED CORN SALAD

MAKES 6 SERVINGS

- 3 tablespoons lime juice
- ½ teaspoon salt
- ¼ cup extra virgin olive oil
- 4 to 6 ears corn, husked (enough to make 3 to 4 cups kernels)
- ⅔ cup canned black beans, rinsed and drained
- ½ cup chopped fresh cilantro
- 2 teaspoons minced seeded chipotle pepper (about 1 canned chipotle pepper in adobo sauce)

1. Whisk lime juice and salt in small bowl. Gradually whisk in oil until well blended.

2. Cut corn kernels off cobs. Heat large skillet over medium-high heat. Cook corn in single layer 15 to 17 minutes or until browned and tender, stirring frequently. Transfer to medium bowl.

3. Place beans in small microwavable bowl; microwave on HIGH 1 minute or until heated through. Add beans, cilantro and chipotle pepper to corn; mix well.

4. Pour lime juice mixture over corn mixture; stir gently to coat.

TIP

Store leftover chipotle peppers in adobo sauce in a covered food storage container and refrigerate or freeze.

SALMON, ASPARAGUS AND ORZO SALAD

MAKES 4 SERVINGS

- 1 salmon fillet (about 8 ounces)
- 1 cup uncooked orzo pasta
- 8 ounces asparagus, cooked and cut into 2-inch pieces (about 1½ cups)
- ½ cup dried cranberries
- ¼ cup sliced green onions
- 3 tablespoons extra virgin olive oil
- 1 tablespoon white wine vinegar
- 1½ teaspoons Dijon mustard
- ½ teaspoon salt
- ⅛ teaspoon black pepper

1. Prepare grill for direct cooking. Grill salmon on oiled grid over medium heat about 10 minutes per inch of thickness or until opaque in center. Remove to plate; let cool. Flake salmon into bite-size pieces.

2. Meanwhile, cook orzo according to package directions; drain and cool.

3. Combine salmon, orzo, asparagus, cranberries and green onions in large bowl. Whisk oil, vinegar, mustard, salt and pepper in small bowl until well blended.

4. Pour dressing over salmon mixture; toss gently to coat. Refrigerate 30 minutes to 1 hour before serving.

ROASTED CAULIFLOWER SALAD IN PITAS

MAKES 6 SERVINGS

1 large head cauliflower (2½ pounds), cut into 1-inch florets

2 tablespoons olive oil

¾ teaspoon salt, divided

¼ teaspoon black pepper

½ cup mayonnaise

¼ cup plain Greek yogurt

1 teaspoon cider vinegar

1 teaspoon Dijon mustard

1 cup red grapes, halved

2 tablespoons minced fresh chives

½ cup chopped walnuts, toasted

Pita bread rounds

Lettuce or microgreens

1. Preheat oven to 425°F. Place cauliflower on baking sheet. Drizzle with oil and sprinkle with ½ teaspoon salt and pepper; toss to coat.

2. Roast 45 minutes or until cauliflower is well browned and very tender. Cool completely.

3. Whisk mayonnaise, yogurt, vinegar, mustard and remaining ¼ teaspoon salt in large bowl until well blended. Stir in grapes, chives and roasted cauliflower. Fold in walnuts.

4. Serve in pita rounds with lettuce.

SOUPS

WEST AFRICAN PEANUT SOUP

MAKES 6 TO 8 SERVINGS

- 2 tablespoons coconut oil
- 1 large onion, chopped
- ½ cup chopped roasted peanuts
- 1½ tablespoons minced fresh ginger
- 4 cloves garlic, minced (about 1 tablespoon)
- 1 teaspoon salt
- 4 cups vegetable broth
- 2 sweet potatoes, peeled and cut into ½-inch cubes
- 1 can (28 ounces) whole tomatoes, drained and coarsely chopped
- ¼ teaspoon ground red pepper
- 1 bunch Swiss chard or kale, stemmed and shredded
- ⅓ cup unsweetened peanut butter (creamy or chunky)

1. Heat oil in large saucepan over medium-high heat. Add onion; cook and stir 5 minutes or until softened. Add peanuts, ginger, garlic and salt; cook and stir 1 minute.

2. Stir in broth, sweet potatoes, tomatoes and red pepper; bring to a boil. Reduce heat to medium; simmer 10 minutes.

3. Stir in kale and peanut butter; cook over medium-low heat 10 minutes or until vegetables are tender and soup is creamy.

LENTIL SOUP

MAKES 6 TO 8 SERVINGS

- 2 tablespoons olive oil, divided
- 2 medium onions, chopped
- 1½ teaspoons salt
- 4 cloves garlic, minced
- ¼ cup tomato paste
- 1 teaspoon dried oregano
- ½ teaspoon dried basil
- ¼ teaspoon dried thyme
- ¼ teaspoon black pepper
- ½ cup dry sherry or white wine
- 8 cups vegetable broth
- 2 cups water
- 3 carrots, cut into ½-inch pieces
- 2 cups dried lentils, rinsed and sorted
- 1 cup chopped fresh parsley
- 1 tablespoon balsamic vinegar

1. Heat 1 tablespoon oil in large saucepan or Dutch oven over medium heat. Add onions; cook 10 minutes, stirring occasionally. Add remaining 1 tablespoon oil and salt; cook 10 minutes or until onions are golden brown, stirring frequently.

2. Add garlic; cook and stir 1 minute. Add tomato paste, oregano, basil, thyme and pepper; cook and stir 1 minute. Stir in sherry; cook 30 seconds, scraping up browned bits from bottom of saucepan.

3. Stir in broth, water, carrots and lentils; cover and bring to a boil over high heat. Reduce heat to medium-low; cook, partially covered, 30 minutes or until lentils are tender.

4. Remove from heat; stir in parsley and vinegar.

SPICY SQUASH AND CHICKEN SOUP

MAKES 4 SERVINGS

- 1 tablespoon olive oil
- 1 small onion, finely chopped
- 1 stalk celery, finely chopped
- 2 cups cubed butternut or delicata squash (about 1 small)
- 2 cups chicken broth
- 1 can (about 14 ounces) diced tomatoes with green chiles
- 1 cup chopped cooked chicken
- ¾ teaspoon salt
- ½ teaspoon ground ginger
- ⅛ teaspoon ground cumin
- ⅛ teaspoon black pepper
- 2 teaspoons lime juice
- Sprigs fresh parsley or cilantro (optional)

1. Heat oil in large saucepan over medium heat. Add onion and celery; cook and stir 5 minutes or until vegetables are tender. Stir in squash, broth, tomatoes, chicken, salt, ginger, cumin and pepper; bring to a boil.

2. Reduce heat to low; cover and simmer 30 minutes or until squash is tender. Stir in lime juice; sprinkle with parsley.

TIP

Delicata is an elongated, creamy yellow winter squash with green striations and hard skin. To use, cut the squash lengthwise, scoop out the seeds, peel and cut into cubes.

HOT AND SOUR SOUP WITH BOK CHOY AND TOFU

MAKES 4 SERVINGS

- 1 tablespoon dark sesame oil
- 4 ounces fresh shiitake mushrooms, stems finely chopped, caps thinly sliced
- 2 cloves garlic, minced
- 2 cups mushroom broth or vegetable broth
- 1 cup plus 2 tablespoons cold water, divided
- 2 tablespoons reduced-sodium soy sauce
- 1½ tablespoons rice vinegar or white wine vinegar
- ¼ teaspoon red pepper flakes
- 1½ tablespoons cornstarch
- 2 cups coarsely chopped bok choy leaves or napa cabbage
- 10 ounces silken extra firm tofu, well drained, cut into ½-inch cubes
- 1 green onion, thinly sliced

1. Heat oil in large saucepan over medium heat. Add mushrooms and garlic; cook and stir 3 minutes. Add broth, 1 cup water, soy sauce, vinegar and red pepper flakes; bring to a boil. Simmer 5 minutes.

2. Whisk remaining 2 tablespoons water into cornstarch in small bowl until smooth. Stir into soup; cook 2 minutes or until thickened.

3. Stir in bok choy; cook 2 to 3 minutes or until wilted. Stir in tofu; cook until heated through. Sprinkle with green onion just before serving.

FRENCH PEASANT SOUP

MAKES 2 SERVINGS

- 1 slice bacon, chopped
- ½ cup diced carrot
- ½ cup diced celery
- ¼ cup minced onion
- 1 clove garlic, minced
- 2 tablespoons dry white wine or water
- 1 can (about 14 ounces) vegetable broth
- 1 bay leaf
- 1 sprig fresh parsley *or* 1 teaspoon dried parsley flakes
- 1 sprig fresh thyme *or* 1 teaspoon dried thyme
- ½ cup chopped green beans (½-inch pieces)
- 2 tablespoons uncooked small pasta or elbow macaroni
- ½ cup canned cannellini beans, rinsed and drained
- ½ cup diced zucchini
- ¼ cup chopped leek
- 2 teaspoons prepared pesto

  Grated Parmesan cheese

1. Cook bacon in medium saucepan over medium heat 3 minutes or until partially cooked. Add carrot, celery, onion and garlic; cook 5 minutes or until carrots are crisp-tender. Stir in wine; cook until most of wine has evaporated. Add broth, bay leaf, parsley and thyme; cook 10 minutes.

2. Add green beans to saucepan; cook 5 minutes. Add pasta; cook 5 to 7 minutes or until almost tender. Add cannellini beans, zucchini and leek; cook 3 to 5 minutes or until vegetables are tender.

3. Remove and discard bay leaf and herb sprigs. Ladle soup into two bowls. Stir 1 teaspoon pesto into each bowl; sprinkle with cheese.

TIP

For a vegetarian version, simply omit the bacon. Use 1 tablespoon olive oil to cook the vegetables in step 1.

MIDDLE EASTERN CHICKEN SOUP

MAKES 4 SERVINGS

3 cups water

1 can (about 15 ounces) chickpeas, rinsed and drained

1 can (about 14 ounces) chicken broth

1 cup chopped cooked chicken

1 small onion, chopped

1 carrot, chopped

1 clove garlic, minced

1 teaspoon dried oregano

1 teaspoon ground cumin

½ teaspoon salt

½ (10-ounce) package fresh spinach, stemmed and coarsely chopped

⅛ teaspoon black pepper

1. Combine water, chickpeas, broth, chicken, onion, carrot, garlic, oregano, cumin and salt in medium saucepan; bring to a boil over high heat. Reduce heat to medium-low; cover and simmer 15 minutes.

2. Stir in spinach and pepper; simmer, uncovered, 2 minutes or just until spinach is wilted.

VEGETABLE AND RED LENTIL SOUP

MAKES 4 SERVINGS

- 1 can (about 14 ounces) vegetable broth
- 1 can (about 14 ounces) diced tomatoes
- 2 medium zucchini or yellow summer squash (or 1 of each), chopped
- 1 red or yellow bell pepper, chopped
- ½ cup thinly sliced carrots
- ½ cup dried red lentils, rinsed and sorted
- ½ teaspoon salt
- ½ teaspoon sugar
- ¼ teaspoon black pepper
- 2 tablespoons chopped fresh basil or thyme
- ½ cup croutons (optional)

SLOW COOKER DIRECTIONS

1. Combine broth, tomatoes, zucchini, bell pepper, carrots, lentils, salt, sugar and black pepper in slow cooker; mix well.

2. Cover; cook on LOW 8 hours or on HIGH 4 hours. Top with basil and croutons, if desired.

CURRIED PARSNIP SOUP

MAKES 6 TO 8 SERVINGS

3 pounds parsnips, peeled and cut into 2-inch pieces

1 tablespoon olive oil

2 tablespoons butter

1 medium yellow onion, chopped

2 stalks celery, diced

1 tablespoon salt

3 cloves garlic, minced

1 to 2 teaspoons curry powder

½ teaspoon grated fresh ginger

½ teaspoon black pepper

8 cups reduced-sodium chicken broth

Toasted bread slices (optional)

Chopped fresh chives (optional)

1. Preheat oven to 400°F. Line baking sheet with foil.

2. Combine parsnips and oil in large bowl; toss to coat. Spread in single layer on prepared baking sheet. Bake 35 to 45 minutes or until parsnips are tender and lightly browned around edges, stirring once halfway through cooking.

3. Melt butter in large saucepan or Dutch oven over medium heat. Add onion and celery; cook and stir about 8 minutes or until vegetables are tender and onion is translucent. Add salt, garlic, curry powder, ginger and pepper; cook and stir 1 minute. Add parsnips and broth; bring to a boil over medium-high heat. Reduce heat to medium-low; cover and simmer 10 minutes.

4. Working in batches, blend soup in blender or food processor until smooth. (Or use hand-held immersion blender.) Transfer blended soup to large bowl. Serve with toasted bread, if desired; garnish with chives.

CHICKPEA-VEGETABLE SOUP

MAKES 4 SERVINGS

1 teaspoon olive oil

1 cup chopped onion

½ cup chopped green bell pepper

2 cloves garlic, minced

2 cans (about 14 ounces each) chopped tomatoes

3 cups water

2 cups broccoli florets

1 can (about 15 ounces) chickpeas, rinsed, drained and slightly mashed

½ cup (3 ounces) uncooked orzo or rosamarina pasta

1 bay leaf

1 tablespoon chopped fresh thyme *or* 1 teaspoon dried thyme

1 tablespoon chopped fresh rosemary *or* 1 teaspoon dried rosemary

1 tablespoon lime or lemon juice

1 teaspoon salt

½ teaspoon ground turmeric

¼ teaspoon ground red pepper

¼ cup pumpkin seeds or sunflower kernels

1. Heat oil in large saucepan over medium heat. Add onion, bell pepper and garlic; cook and stir 5 minutes or until vegetables are tender.

2. Add tomatoes, water, broccoli, chickpeas, orzo, bay leaf, thyme, rosemary, lime juice, salt, turmeric and ground red pepper; bring to a boil over high heat. Reduce heat to medium-low; cover and simmer 10 to 12 minutes or until orzo is tender.

3. Remove and discard bay leaf. Sprinkle with pumpkin seeds just before serving.

SOUTHWEST CORN AND TURKEY SOUP

MAKES 6 SERVINGS

- 2 dried ancho chiles (about 4 inches long) *or* 6 dried New Mexico chiles (about 6 inches long)
- 1 tablespoon olive oil
- 1 medium onion, thinly sliced
- 3 cloves garlic, minced
- 1 teaspoon ground cumin
- 3 cans (about 14 ounces each) chicken broth
- 2 small zucchini, cut into ½-inch slices
- 1½ to 2 cups shredded cooked turkey
- 1 can (about 15 ounces) black beans or chickpeas, rinsed and drained
- 1 package (10 ounces) frozen corn
- ¼ cup yellow cornmeal
- 1 teaspoon dried oregano
- ½ teaspoon salt
- ⅓ cup chopped fresh cilantro

1. Cut stems from chiles; remove and discard seeds. Place chiles in medium bowl; cover with boiling water. Let stand 20 to 40 minutes or until chiles are softened.

2. Drain chiles; cut open lengthwise and lay flat on work surface. Scrape chile pulp from skin with edge of small knife. Finely mince pulp.

3. Heat oil in large saucepan over medium heat. Add onion; cook and stir 3 to 4 minutes. Add garlic and cumin; cook and stir 30 seconds. Stir in broth, reserved chile pulp, zucchini, turkey, beans, corn, cornmeal, oregano and salt; bring to a boil over high heat. Reduce heat to low; simmer 15 minutes or until zucchini is tender.

4. Stir in cilantro just before serving.

TIP

This soup can be easily adapted to whatever poultry or meat you have on hand. Instead of turkey, use grilled or rotisserie chicken or leftover pork. For vegetarians, simply replace the turkey with an additional can of beans and use vegetable broth instead of chicken broth.

MISO SOUP WITH TOFU

MAKES 4 SERVINGS

½ **cup dried bonito flakes***

4 **cups chicken broth**

2 **teaspoons vegetable oil**

1 **leek, white part only, finely chopped**

1 **tablespoon white miso****

8 **ounces firm tofu, cut into ½-inch cubes (about 1½ cups)**

*Dried bonito flakes (katsuobushi) are avaliable in the Asian section of large supermarkets or in Asian stores.
**Miso is a fermented soybean paste used frequently in Japanese cooking. The light yellow variety, usually labeled "white," is the mildest. Look for it in tubs or plastic pouches in the produce section or Asian aisle of the supermarket.

1. Combine bonito flakes and broth in medium saucepan; bring to a boil over medium-high heat. Strain out and discard bonito, reserving broth.

2. Heat oil in medium saucepan over medium heat. Add leek; cook 2 to 3 minutes or until tender, stirring frequently.

3. Return broth to saucepan. Add miso; mix well. Add tofu; cook over low heat just until heated through.

COCONUT CAULIFLOWER CREAM SOUP

MAKES 4 TO 6 SERVINGS

- 1 tablespoon coconut oil
- 1 medium onion, chopped
- 1 tablespoon minced garlic
- 1 tablespoon minced fresh ginger
- 1 teaspoon salt
- 1 head cauliflower (1½ pounds), cut into florets
- 2 cans (about 13 ounces each) coconut milk, divided
- 1 cup water
- 1 teaspoon garam masala
- ½ teaspoon ground turmeric
- Chopped fresh cilantro (optional)
- Pinch ground red pepper and/or hot chili oil (optional)

1. Heat oil in large saucepan over medium-high heat. Add onion; cook and stir 5 minutes or until softened. Add garlic, ginger and salt; cook and stir 30 seconds.

2. Add cauliflower, 1 can of coconut milk, water, garam masala and turmeric. Reduce heat to medium; cover and simmer 20 minutes or until cauliflower is very tender.

3. Remove from heat; blend soup with immersion blender until smooth.

4. Return saucepan to medium heat. Add 1 cup additional coconut milk; cook and stir until heated through. Add additional coconut milk, if desired, to reach desired consistency. Garnish with cilantro, red pepper and/or chili oil.

CHICKEN, BARLEY AND VEGETABLE SOUP

MAKES 6 SERVINGS

6 ounces boneless skinless chicken breasts, cut into ½-inch pieces

6 ounces boneless skinless chicken thighs, cut into ½-inch pieces

1 teaspoon salt

¼ teaspoon black pepper

1 tablespoon olive oil

½ cup uncooked pearl barley

4 cans (about 14 ounces each) chicken broth

2 cups water

1 bay leaf

2 cups baby carrots

2 cups diced peeled potatoes

2 cups sliced mushrooms

2 cups frozen peas

3 tablespoons sour cream

1 tablespoon chopped fresh dill *or* 1 teaspoon dried dill weed

1. Sprinkle chicken with salt and pepper. Heat oil in large saucepan over medium-high heat. Add chicken; cook 2 minutes or until lightly browned. Turn chicken; cook 2 minutes. Remove to plate.

2. Add barley to saucepan; cook and stir 1 to 2 minutes or until barley begins to brown, adding 1 tablespoon broth if needed to prevent burning. Add remaining broth, water and bay leaf; bring to a boil. Reduce heat to low; cover and simmer 30 minutes.

3. Add chicken, carrots, potatoes and mushrooms to saucepan; cook 10 minutes or until vegetables are tender, stirring occasionally. Add peas; cook 2 minutes. Remove and discard bay leaf.

4. Top with sour cream and dill; serve immediately.

PASTA & NOODLES

CILANTRO PEANUT PESTO ON SOBA

MAKES 4 TO 6 SERVINGS (1 CUP PESTO)

- 1 **cup packed fresh basil leaves**
- ½ **cup packed fresh cilantro**
- ¾ **cup dry roasted peanuts, divided**
- 1 **jalapeño pepper, seeded**
- 3 **cloves garlic**
- 2 **teaspoons soy sauce**
- 1 **tablespoon plus ¾ teaspoon salt, divided**
- ½ **cup peanut oil**
- 1 **package (about 12 ounces) uncooked soba noodles**
- **Chopped fresh cilantro**

1. Combine basil, ½ cup cilantro, ½ cup peanuts, jalapeño, garlic, soy sauce and ¾ teaspoon salt in food processor; pulse until coarsely chopped. With motor running, drizzle in oil in thin, steady stream; process until well blended.

2. Bring large saucepan of water to a boil. Add remaining 1 tablespoon salt; stir until dissolved. Add noodles; return to a boil. Reduce heat to low; cook 3 minutes or until tender. Drain and rinse under cold water to cool.

3. Place noodles in medium bowl; stir in pesto. Chop remaining ¼ cup peanuts; sprinkle over noodles. Garnish with chopped cilantro.

PASTA WITH TUNA, GREEN BEANS AND TOMATOES

MAKES 6 SERVINGS

- **8** ounces uncooked whole wheat penne, rigatoni or fusilli pasta
- **1½** cups frozen cut green beans
- **2** tablespoons olive oil, divided
- **3** green onions, sliced
- **1** clove garlic, minced
- **1** can (about 14 ounces) diced Italian-style tomatoes, drained *or 2 large tomatoes, chopped (about 2 cups)*
- **½** teaspoon salt
- **½** teaspoon Italian seasoning
- **¼** teaspoon black pepper
- **1** can (12 ounces) solid albacore tuna packed in water, drained and flaked
- Chopped fresh parsley (optional)

1. Cook pasta according to package directions, adding green beans during last 7 minutes of cooking time. Drain and keep warm.

2. Meanwhile, heat 1 tablespoon oil in large skillet over medium heat. Add green onions and garlic; cook and stir 2 minutes. Add tomatoes, salt, Italian seasoning and pepper; cook and stir 4 to 5 minutes.

3. Gently stir in pasta mixture, tuna and remaining 1 tablespoon oil; cook 1 minute or until heated through. Garnish with parsley.

SUMMER'S BOUNTY PASTA WITH BROCCOLI PESTO

MAKES 4 SERVINGS

2 cups broccoli florets

2 cups uncooked bowtie (farfalle) pasta

½ cup loosely packed fresh basil leaves

5 tablespoons shredded Parmesan-Romano cheese blend, divided

3 tablespoons extra virgin olive oil, divided

2 tablespoons chopped walnuts, toasted*

2 cloves garlic, crushed, divided

¼ teaspoon salt

6 ounces medium cooked shrimp

¼ teaspoon black pepper

1 package (about 5 ounces) baby spinach

1 cup halved grape tomatoes

*To toast walnuts, cook in small skillet over medium heat 1 to 2 minutes or until lightly browned, stirring frequently.

1. Bring large saucepan of water to a boil. Add broccoli; cook 3 minutes or until tender. Remove to small bowl with slotted spoon; reserve cooking water.

2. Cook pasta according to package directions using reserved water. Drain pasta and return to saucepan; cover to keep warm.

3. Combine broccoli, basil, 3 tablespoons cheese, 2 tablespoons oil, walnuts, 1 clove garlic and salt in food processor or blender; process until smooth. Stir into pasta in saucepan; toss to coat. Cover to keep warm.

4. Heat remaining 1 tablespoon oil in large skillet over medium heat. Add shrimp, remaining 1 clove garlic and pepper; cook and stir until heated through. Stir in spinach and tomatoes; cook until spinach is wilted and tomatoes begin to soften. Add to pasta; stir gently to combine.

5. Divide pasta mixture evenly among four serving bowls; top with remaining 2 tablespoons cheese.

PUTTANESCA WITH ANGEL HAIR PASTA

MAKES 4 TO 6 SERVINGS

- 2 tablespoons olive oil
- 2 to 3 anchovy fillets, chopped
- 3 cloves garlic, minced
- 2 tablespoons tomato paste
- 2 cans (about 14 ounces each) diced tomatoes
- 1 teaspoon dried oregano
- 1 teaspoon dried basil
  Salt and black pepper
- 1 can (15 ounces) tomato sauce
- ½ cup pitted Greek olives, coarsely chopped
- 2 tablespoons capers, rinsed and drained
- ½ to 1 teaspoon red pepper flakes (to taste)
- 1 pound uncooked fresh or dried angel hair pasta

1. Heat oil in large skillet over medium-low heat. Add anchovies; cook 3 minutes, stirring occasionally. Add garlic; cook and stir 3 minutes or until lightly browned. Add tomato paste; cook 2 minutes, stirring occasionally.

2. Stir in tomatoes, oregano, basil, salt and black pepper; cook over medium heat about 30 minutes or until tomatoes break down and mixture becomes saucy, stirring occasionally.

3. Reduce heat to medium-low. Stir in tomato sauce, olives, capers and red pepper flakes; cook 10 minutes.

4. Meanwhile, bring large saucepan of salted water to a boil over high heat. Cook pasta according to package directions. Drain pasta; toss with sauce.

PASTA E CECI

MAKES 4 SERVINGS

- 4 tablespoons olive oil, divided
- 1 onion, chopped
- 1 carrot, chopped
- 1 clove garlic, minced
- 1 sprig fresh rosemary
- 1 teaspoon salt
- 1 can (28 ounces) whole tomatoes, drained and crushed (see Tip)
- 2 cups vegetable broth or water
- 1 can (about 15 ounces) chickpeas, undrained
- 1 bay leaf
- ⅛ teaspoon red pepper flakes
- 1 cup uncooked orecchiette pasta
- Black pepper
- Chopped fresh parsley or basil

1. Heat 3 tablespoons oil in large saucepan over medium-high heat. Add onion and carrot; cook 8 minutes or until vegetables are softened, stirring occasionally.

2. Add garlic, rosemary and salt; cook and stir 1 minute. Stir in tomatoes, broth, chickpeas with liquid, bay leaf and red pepper flakes; mix well. Remove 1 cup mixture to food processor or blender; process until smooth. Stir back into saucepan; bring to a boil.

3. Stir in pasta. Reduce heat to medium; cook 12 to 15 minutes or until pasta is tender and mixture is creamy. Remove and discard bay leaf and rosemary sprig. Taste and season with additional salt and black pepper, if desired. Divide among bowls; garnish with parsley and drizzle with remaining 1 tablespoon oil.

TIP

To crush the tomatoes, take them out of the can one at a time and crush them between your fingers over the pot. Or coarsely chop them with a knife.

ZUCCHINI NOODLE PAD THAI

MAKES 4 SERVINGS

1¾ cups water

3 tablespoons date sugar or packed brown sugar

3 tablespoons soy sauce

2 tablespoons lime juice

1 tablespoon anchovy paste *or* 2 tablespoons fish sauce

2 large zucchini, spiraled into thin strips *or* about 6 cups (24 ounces) prepared zucchini noodles

4 tablespoons grapeseed oil, divided

1 package (14 ounces) firm tofu, pressed and cut into strips or cubes

2 eggs, lightly beaten

2 cloves garlic, minced

1 tablespoon paprika

¼ to ½ teaspoon ground red pepper

8 ounces fresh bean sprouts, divided

½ cup coarsely chopped unsalted dry-roasted peanuts

4 green onions, cut into 1-inch pieces

½ lime, cut into 4 wedges (optional)

1. Combine water, date sugar, soy sauce, lime juice and anchovy paste in small bowl; mix well.

2. Cut zucchini noodles into desired lengths. Heat 1 tablespoon oil in wok over medium-high heat. Add zucchini; stir-fry 2 to 3 minutes or until crisp-tender. Transfer to large bowl.

3. Heat 1 tablespoon oil in wok over medium-high heat. Add tofu; cook about 5 minutes or until browned on all sides, turning occasionally. Transfer to bowl with zucchini.

4. Heat wok over medium heat about 30 seconds or until hot. Drizzle 1 tablespoon oil into wok and heat 15 seconds. Add eggs; cook 1 minute or just until set on bottom. Turn eggs over and stir to scramble until cooked but not dry. Transfer to bowl with zucchini.

5. Drizzle remaining 1 tablespoon oil into wok and heat 15 seconds. Add garlic, paprika and red pepper; cook 30 seconds or until fragrant. Add zucchini, tofu, egg and sauce mixture; stir-fry 3 to 5 minutes or until zucchini is tender and coated with sauce. Stir in bean sprouts, peanuts and green onions; cook about 1 minute or until green onions begin to wilt. Serve immediately with lime wedges, if desired.

LENTIL BOLOGNESE

MAKES 6 TO 8 SERVINGS

- 2 **tablespoons olive oil**
- 1 **onion, chopped**
- 1 **carrot, chopped**
- 1 **stalk celery, chopped**
- 2 **cloves garlic, minced**
- 1 **teaspoon salt**
- ½ **teaspoon dried oregano**

  Pinch red pepper flakes

- 3 **tablespoons tomato paste**
- ¼ **cup dry white wine**
- 1 **can (28 ounces) crushed tomatoes**
- 1 **can (14 ounces) diced tomatoes**
- 1 **cup dried lentils, rinsed and sorted**
- 1 **portobello mushroom, gills removed, finely chopped**
- 1½ **cups water or vegetable broth**

  Hot cooked pasta

1. Heat oil in large saucepan over medium heat. Add onion, carrot and celery; cook and stir 10 minutes or until onion is lightly browned and carrots are softened.

2. Stir in garlic, salt, oregano and red pepper flakes. Add tomato paste; cook and stir 1 minute. Add wine; cook and stir until absorbed. Stir in crushed tomatoes, diced tomatoes, lentils, mushroom and water; bring to a simmer.

3. Reduce heat to medium; partially cover and simmer about 20 minutes. Uncover; simmer 20 minutes or until lentils are tender. Serve over pasta.

BOWTIE PASTA WITH CHICKEN AND ROASTED GARLIC

MAKES 6 SERVINGS

1 head garlic

3 tablespoons plus 1 teaspoon olive oil, divided

1½ pounds assorted wild mushrooms (such as shiitake, portobello or cremini), sliced

1 can (about 14 ounces) diced tomatoes, undrained

¾ cup chopped green onions

1½ cups chicken broth

1 pound cooked boneless skinless chicken breasts and/or thighs, diced

¼ cup chopped fresh basil

2 teaspoons salt

1 teaspoon black pepper

1 pound bowtie (farfalle) pasta, cooked and drained

1. Preheat oven to 325°F. Cut off ¼ inch of garlic top; rub exposed cloves with 1 teaspoon oil. Wrap garlic in foil, roast 45 minutes. Let stand until cool enough to handle. Squeeze garlic pulp into small bowl.

2. Heat remaining 3 tablespoons oil in large skillet over high heat. Add mushrooms; cook and stir 3 minutes. Add tomatoes and green onions; cook and stir 2 minutes. Add broth, scraping up browned bits from bottom of skillet. Cook 5 minutes or until broth reduces to 1 cup. Add garlic, chicken, basil, salt and pepper; cook and stir 2 minutes or until heated through.

3. Combine sauce and pasta in large bowl; stir gently to blend.

TIP

It's simple to turn this dish into a vegetarian favorite. Replace the chicken with 1 package (5 to 6 ounces) baby spinach and use vegetable broth instead of chicken broth. Proceed as directed in step 2.

SESAME NOODLE BOWL

MAKES 6 SERVINGS

1 package (16 ounces) uncooked spaghetti

6 tablespoons soy sauce

5 tablespoons dark sesame oil

3 tablespoons sugar

3 tablespoons rice vinegar

4 tablespoons grapeseed oil, divided

3 cloves garlic, minced

1 teaspoon grated fresh ginger or ginger paste

½ teaspoon sriracha sauce

2 green onions, sliced

1 red bell pepper

1 cucumber

1 carrot

1 package (14 to 16 ounces) firm tofu, drained and patted dry

Sesame seeds (optional)

1. Cook spaghetti according to package directions in large saucepan of boiling salted water until al dente. Drain pasta, reserving 1 tablespoon cooking water.

2. Whisk soy sauce, sesame oil, sugar, vinegar, 2 tablespoons grapeseed oil, garlic, ginger and sriracha in large bowl. Stir in noodles, reserved pasta cooking water and green onions. Let stand at least 30 minutes until noodles have cooled to room temperature and most of sauce is absorbed, stirring occasionally.

3. Meanwhile, cut bell pepper into thin strips. Peel cucumber and carrot and shred with julienne peeler into long strands, or cut into thin strips.

4. Cut tofu into thin triangles or 1-inch cubes. Heat remaining 2 tablespoons grapeseed oil in large nonstick skillet over high heat. Add tofu; cook 5 minutes or until browned on all sides, turning occasionally.

5. Place noodles in bowls; top with tofu, bell pepper, cucumber and carrot. Sprinkle with sesame seeds, if desired.

NOTE

Sesame noodles can be served warm or cold. To serve them cold, cover and refrigerate a few hours or overnight after mixing the noodles with the sauce. Prepare the vegetables and tofu just before serving.

LEMON SALMON AND SPINACH PASTA

MAKES 4 SERVINGS

- 12 ounces salmon fillet
- 8 ounces uncooked fettuccine
- 2 tablespoons butter
- 2 cloves garlic, minced
- 1 teaspoon finely grated lemon peel
- ½ teaspoon salt
- ¼ teaspoon red pepper flakes
- 2 tablespoons lemon juice
- 3 cups baby spinach
- ½ cup shredded carrot

1. Pat salmon dry with paper towels; remove and discard skin. Cut fish into ½-inch pieces.

2. Cook fettuccine according to package directions; drain and return to saucepan.

3. Meanwhile, melt butter in large skillet over medium-high heat. Add salmon, garlic, lemon peel, salt and red pepper flakes; cook 4 to 7 minutes or until salmon begins to flake when tested with fork. Gently stir in lemon juice.

4. Add salmon mixture, spinach and carrot to hot cooked fettuccine; gently toss to combine. Serve immediately.

KOSHARI

MAKES 6 TO 8 SERVINGS

- **5** cups water
- **1** cup white basmati rice, rinsed and drained
- **1** cup brown lentils, rinsed and sorted
- **3** teaspoons kosher salt, divided
- **1** teaspoon ground cinnamon, divided
- **½** teaspoon ground nutmeg, divided
- **1** cup uncooked elbow macaroni
- **¼** cup olive oil
- **1** large onion, thinly sliced
- **1** large onion, diced
- **1** tablespoon minced garlic
- **1** teaspoon ground cumin
- **½** teaspoon ground coriander
- **¼** teaspoon red pepper flakes
- **¼** teaspoon black pepper
- **1** can (28 ounces) crushed tomatoes
- **2** teaspoons red wine vinegar

1. Bring water to a boil in large saucepan. Stir in rice, lentils, 2 teaspoons salt, ½ teaspoon cinnamon and ¼ teaspoon nutmeg; mix well. Reduce heat to medium; simmer, partially covered, 7 minutes. Stir in macaroni; cover and cook 8 minutes. Remove from heat. Place clean kitchen towel over top of saucepan. Cover with lid and let stand 10 minutes.

2. Meanwhile, heat oil in large skillet over medium-high heat. Add sliced onion; cook 12 minutes or until edges are dark brown and onion is softened. Transfer to medium bowl with slotted spoon, leaving oil in skillet. Season with ¼ teaspoon salt. Set aside.

3. Heat same skillet with oil over medium heat. Add diced onion; cook 8 minutes or until softened, stirring occasionally. Add garlic, cumin, coriander, remaining ½ teaspoon cinnamon, red pepper flakes, black pepper and remaining ¼ teaspoon nutmeg; cook 30 seconds or until fragrant. Add tomatoes, vinegar and remaining ¾ teaspoon salt; cook 8 to 10 minutes or until thickened, stirring occasionally.

4. Fluff rice mixture lightly before scooping into individual bowls. Top each serving with tomato sauce and reserved onions.

COLD PEANUT NOODLE AND EDAMAME SALAD

MAKES 4 SERVINGS

- ½ **(8-ounce) package brown rice pad thai noodles**
- 3 **tablespoons soy sauce**
- 2 **tablespoons dark sesame oil**
- 2 **tablespoons unseasoned rice vinegar**
- 1 **tablespoon sugar**
- 1 **tablespoon finely grated fresh ginger**
- 1 **tablespoon creamy peanut butter**
- 1 **tablespoon sriracha or hot chili sauce**
- 2 **teaspoons minced garlic**
- ½ **cup thawed frozen shelled edamame**
- ¼ **cup shredded carrots**
- ¼ **cup sliced green onions**
- **Chopped peanuts (optional)**

1. Prepare noodles according to package directions for pasta. Rinse under cold water; drain. Cut noodles into 3-inch lengths. Place in large bowl; set aside.

2. Whisk soy sauce, oil, vinegar, sugar, ginger, peanut butter, sriracha and garlic in small bowl until smooth and well blended.

3. Pour dressing over noodles; toss gently to coat. Stir in edamame and carrots. Cover and refrigerate at least 30 minutes before serving. Top with green onions and peanuts, if desired.

NOTE

Brown rice pad thai noodles can be found in the Asian section of the supermarket. Regular thin rice noodles or whole wheat spaghetti may be substituted.

BOWLS

PUMPKIN CURRY

MAKES 4 SERVINGS

- 1 tablespoon coconut oil
- 1 package (14 ounces) firm tofu, drained, patted dry and cut into 1-inch cubes
- ¼ cup Thai red curry paste
- 2 cloves garlic, minced
- 1 can (15 ounces) pure pumpkin
- 1 can (13 ounces) coconut milk
- 1 cup vegetable broth or water
- 1½ teaspoons salt
- 1 teaspoon sriracha sauce
- 4 cups cut-up fresh vegetables (broccoli, cauliflower, red bell pepper and/or sweet potato)
- ½ cup peas

  Hot cooked rice
- ¼ cup shredded fresh basil (optional)

1. Heat oil in wok or large skillet over high heat. Add tofu; stir-fry 5 minutes or until lightly browned. Add curry paste and garlic; cook and stir 1 minute or until tofu is coated.

2. Add pumpkin, coconut milk, broth, salt and sriracha; bring to a boil. Stir in vegetables. Reduce heat to medium; cover and simmer 20 minutes or until vegetables are tender.

3. Stir in peas; cook 1 minute or until heated through. Serve over rice; top with basil, if desired.

BIBIMBAP WITH CAULIFLOWER RICE

MAKES 4 TO 6 SERVINGS

- 3 tablespoons soy sauce, divided
- 1 tablespoon packed brown sugar
- 1½ teaspoons dark sesame oil
- 3 cloves garlic, minced, divided
- 12 ounces beef for stir-fry
- 1 seedless cucumber, thinly sliced
- ⅓ cup rice vinegar
- ¼ teaspoon plus ⅛ teaspoon salt, divided
- 2 tablespoons plus 1 teaspoon grapeseed oil, divided
- 4 ounces shiitake mushrooms, stemmed and thinly sliced
- 3 cups fresh spinach
- 1 tablespoon water
- 3 cups frozen cauliflower rice, cooked according to package directions
- 1 carrot, julienned
- 4 eggs, cooked sunny side up or over easy
- Gochujang sauce or sriracha sauce

1. Combine 2 tablespoons soy sauce, brown sugar, sesame oil and 1 clove garlic in medium bowl. Add beef; stir to coat with marinade. Refrigerate 30 minutes to 1 hour.

2. Combine cucumber, vinegar and ⅛ teaspoon salt in large bowl; mix well. Let stand at room temperature until ready to serve.

3. Heat 1 tablespoon grapeseed oil in medium skillet over high heat. Add mushrooms and remaining ¼ teaspoon salt; cook and stir 3 minutes or until mushrooms are browned and tender. Transfer to medium bowl.

4. Heat 1 teaspoon grapeseed oil in same skillet over high heat. Add spinach and water; cook just until spinach is wilted. Add remaining 2 cloves garlic; cook 30 seconds or until garlic is lightly browned. Stir in remaining 1 tablespoon soy sauce. Transfer spinach to another medium bowl.

5. Heat remaining 1 tablespoon grapeseed oil in same skillet over high heat. Add beef and marinade; cook and stir 2 to 3 minutes or until beef is no longer pink.

6. For each serving, divide cauliflower rice among serving bowls. Top with cucumber, carrot, spinach, mushrooms, beef and egg; serve with desired sauce.

CHICKPEA TIKKA MASALA

MAKES 4 SERVINGS

- 1 tablespoon coconut oil
- 1 onion, chopped
- 3 cloves garlic, minced
- 1 tablespoon minced fresh ginger or ginger paste
- 1 teaspoon salt
- 1 tablespoon garam masala
- 1 teaspoon ground cumin
- 1 teaspoon ground coriander
- ¼ teaspoon ground red pepper
- 2 cans (about 15 ounces each) chickpeas, drained
- 1 can (28 ounces) crushed tomatoes
- 1 can (about 13 ounces) coconut milk
- 1 package (about 12 ounces) firm silken tofu, drained and cut into 1-inch cubes
- Hot cooked rice
- Chopped fresh cilantro (optional)

1. Heat oil in large saucepan over medium-high heat. Add onion; cook and stir 5 minutes or until translucent. Add garlic, ginger, salt, garam masala, cumin, coriander and red pepper; cook and stir 1 minute.

2. Stir in chickpeas, tomatoes and coconut milk; bring to a simmer. Reduce heat to medium-low; cook 30 minutes or until thickened and chickpeas have softened slightly.

3. Gently stir in tofu; cook 7 to 10 minutes or until tofu is heated through. Serve over rice; garnish with cilantro.

SMOKEY CHILI WITH CORN-CILANTRO QUINOA

MAKES 8 SERVINGS

CHILI

- 1 tablespoon grapeseed oil
- 1 pound ground beef or turkey
- 2 cups chopped green bell peppers
- 1 cup chopped onion
- 2 cans (about 14 ounces each) stewed tomatoes
- 2 cans (about 15 ounces each) dark kidney beans, rinsed and drained
- 2½ cups water
- 2 teaspoons smoked paprika
- 3 teaspoons ground cumin, divided
- ½ teaspoon salt

QUINOA

- 1 cup uncooked quinoa, preferably tri-colored
- 1½ cups frozen corn
- ½ cup chopped fresh cilantro
- Salt and black pepper

1. For chili, heat oil in large saucepan or Dutch oven over medium-high heat. Add beef; cook 3 minutes or until beef begins to brown, stirring frequently. Add bell peppers and onion; cook and stir about 6 minutes or until vegetables are tender.

2. Stir in tomatoes, beans, water, paprika, 1 teaspoon cumin and ½ teaspoon salt; bring to a boil. Reduce heat to medium-low; cook, uncovered, 30 minutes or until thickened. Remove from heat, stir in remaining 2 teaspoons cumin.

3. Meanwhile, cook quinoa with corn according to quinoa package directions. Remove from heat; stir in cilantro. Season with salt and black pepper.

4. Spoon quinoa mixture in bowls; top with chili.

CALIFORNIA ROLL FARRO SUSHI BOWL

MAKES 4 SERVINGS

BOWL

- 1 package (8½ ounces) quick-cooking farro
- 2 tablespoons rice vinegar
- 2 tablespoons sugar
- ½ teaspoon salt
- 1 cup shredded carrots
- 2 avocados, sliced
- 2 mini (kirby) cucumbers, thinly sliced
- ¾ pound crab sticks or imitation crab sticks
- 2 teaspoons toasted sesame seeds

DRESSING

- ⅓ cup mayonnaise
- 1 teaspoon sriracha sauce
- 1 teaspoon dark sesame oil
- 1 teaspoon rice vinegar

1. Prepare farro according to package directions.

2. Combine 2 tablespoons rice vinegar, sugar and salt in large microwavable bowl; microwave on HIGH 30 to 45 seconds or until sugar is dissolved. Stir mixture; add farro and toss to coat.

3. Divide farro mixture evenly among four bowls. Top each with equal amount of carrots, avocados, cucumbers and crab sticks. Sprinkle with sesame seeds.

4. Whisk mayonnaise, sriracha, sesame oil and 1 teaspoon rice vinegar in small bowl until well blended. Serve with farro bowls as dressing or dipping sauce.

SPAGHETTI SQUASH WITH SHRIMP AND VEGETABLES

MAKES 4 SERVINGS

- 1 **spaghetti squash (3 pounds)**
- 4 **cups baby spinach**
- 1 **orange or red bell pepper, cut into 1-inch pieces**
- ½ **cup julienned sun-dried tomatoes (not packed in oil)**
- 3 **tablespoons prepared pesto**
- 2 **tablespoons olive oil**
- 1 **teaspoon salt**
- 8 **ounces cooked medium shrimp (with tails on)**
- ¼ **cup grated Parmesan cheese (optional)**

SLOW COOKER DIRECTIONS

1. Pierce squash about 10 times with knife. Place squash in slow cooker; add 1 inch water.

2. Cover; cook on HIGH 2½ hours. Remove squash to large cutting board; let stand until cool enough to handle.

3. Meanwhile, pour off all but 2 tablespoons of water from slow cooker. Add spinach, bell pepper, sun-dried tomatoes, pesto, oil and salt; mix well. Cover; cook on HIGH 5 minutes.

4. Cut squash in half lengthwise. Remove and discard seeds and fibers. Scoop pulp into shreds; stir into spinach mixture in slow cooker. Top with shrimp.

5. Cover; cook on HIGH 15 to 20 minutes or until shrimp are heated through. Serve with cheese, if desired.

SOBA TERIYAKI BOWL

MAKES 4 SERVINGS

- ¾ cup plus 1 tablespoon cornstarch, divided
- 2 teaspoons salt, divided
- ½ cup plus 2 tablespoons water, divided
- 1 head cauliflower, cut into 1-inch florets
- ¾ cup pineapple juice
- ¾ cup soy sauce
- 2 tablespoons date sugar or packed brown sugar
- 1 tablespoon lime juice
- 1 teaspoon minced garlic
- 6 ounces uncooked soba noodles
- 5 cups shredded red, green or mixed cabbage *or* 1 package (14 ounces) coleslaw mix
- ½ cup unseasoned rice vinegar
- 1 teaspoon granulated sugar
- 2 green onions, chopped
- 1 tablespoon sesame seeds

1. Preheat oven to 400°F. Spray baking sheet with nonstick cooking spray. Whisk ¾ cup cornstarch and 1 teaspoon salt in medium bowl. Whisk in ½ cup water until smooth. Dip cauliflower into mixture; place in single layer on prepared baking sheet. Bake 20 minutes or until tender.

2. Meanwhile, combine pineapple juice, soy sauce, date sugar, lime juice and garlic in small saucepan; bring to a simmer over medium heat. Whisk remaining 2 tablespoons water into remaining 1 tablespoon cornstarch in small bowl; stir into sauce. Reduce heat to low; cook and stir 5 minutes. Transfer to large bowl; cool slightly. Remove ¼ cup sauce; set aside.

3. Cook soba noodles according to package directions. Drain and rinse under cold water until cool. Divide among serving bowls.

4. Combine cabbage, vinegar, granulated sugar and remaining 1 teaspoon salt in medium bowl; mix and squeeze with hands until well blended.

5. Add cauliflower to large bowl of sauce; stir to coat. Divide among serving bowls; drizzle with some of reserved sauce. Serve with cabbage mixture; sprinkle with green onions and sesame seeds.

SWEET POTATO AND BLACK BEAN CHIPOTLE CHILI

MAKES 8 TO 10 SERVINGS

1 tablespoon grapeseed oil

2 large onions, diced

1 tablespoon minced garlic

2 tablespoons tomato paste

3 tablespoons chili powder

1 tablespoon chipotle chili powder

1 teaspoon ground cumin

2 teaspoons kosher salt

1 cup water

1 large sweet potato, peeled and cut into ½-inch pieces (about 2 pounds)

2 cans (28 ounces each) black beans, rinsed and drained

2 cans (28 ounces each) crushed tomatoes

Optional toppings: sour cream, sliced green onions, shredded cheddar cheese and/or tortilla chips

SLOW COOKER DIRECTIONS

1. Heat oil in large skillet over medium-high heat. Add onions; cook 8 minutes or until softened and lightly browned. Add garlic, tomato paste, chili powder, chipotle chili powder, cumin and salt; cook and stir 1 minute.

2. Stir in water, scraping up brown bits from bottom of skillet. Transfer to slow cooker; stir in sweet potato, beans and tomatoes.

3. Cover; cook on LOW 8 hours or on HIGH 4 hours. Serve with desired toppings.

PEPPER AND EGG COUSCOUS BOWL

MAKES 4 SERVINGS

1 tablespoon olive oil

3 bell peppers, assorted colors, cut into thin strips

1 red onion

2 cups vegetable broth

1 cup uncooked instant couscous

1 clove garlic, minced

½ teaspoon salt

½ teaspoon dried oregano

½ teaspoon ground cumin

4 to 8 eggs, cooked any style

1 can (about 15 ounces) black beans, rinsed and drained

1 cup grape tomatoes, halved

Crumbled queso fresco, cotija or feta cheese (optional)

1. Heat oil in large skillet over medium-high heat. Add bell peppers and onion; cook and stir 5 minutes or until vegetables are tender.

2. Bring broth to a boil in small saucepan over high heat. Stir in couscous, garlic, salt, oregano and cumin; mix well. Remove from heat; cover and let stand 5 minutes. Fluff with fork.

3. Serve vegetables, eggs and beans over couscous; top with tomatoes and cheese, if desired.

RAINBOW VEGETABLE STEW

MAKES 4 TO 6 SERVINGS

1 tablespoon olive oil

1 red onion, chopped

2 stalks celery, chopped

3 cloves garlic, minced

2 teaspoons salt, divided

4 cups vegetable broth

1 butternut squash (about 2 pounds), peeled and cut into ½-inch pieces

1 red bell pepper, chopped

1 green bell pepper, chopped

1 teaspoon ground cumin

½ teaspoon dried oregano

¼ teaspoon chipotle chili powder

1½ cups water

¾ cup uncooked tricolor or white quinoa

½ cup corn

1 can (about 15 ounces) black beans, rinsed and drained

½ cup chopped fresh parsley

1 tablespoon lime juice

1. Heat oil in large saucepan over medium-high heat. Add onion and celery; cook and stir 5 minutes or until vegetables are softened. Add garlic and 1½ teaspoons salt; cook and stir 30 seconds.

2. Stir in broth, squash, bell peppers, cumin, oregano and chipotle chili powder; bring to a boil. Reduce heat to medium; simmer 20 minutes or until squash is tender.

3. Meanwhile, bring 1½ cups water, quinoa and remaining ½ teaspoon salt to a boil in medium saucepan. Reduce heat to low; cover and cook 15 minutes or until quinoa is tender and water is absorbed.

4. Stir corn and beans into stew; cook 5 minutes or until heated through. Stir in parsley and lime juice. Serve with quinoa.

TURKEY TACO BOWLS

MAKES 4 SERVINGS

1 pound ground turkey

1 package (1 ounce) taco seasoning mix

¾ cup water

1 bag (10 ounces) frozen cauliflower rice

2 cups shredded red cabbage

1 avocado, thinly sliced

2 plum tomatoes, diced

2 green onions, finely chopped

Optional toppings: chopped fresh cilantro, sour cream and crumbled cotija cheese

1. Cook turkey in large nonstick skillet over medium-high heat 6 to 8 minutes or until no longer pink, stirring to break up meat.

2. Stir in taco seasoning mix and water; bring to a boil. Reduce heat to medium-low; cook 5 minutes, stirring occasionally. Set aside.

3. Heat cauliflower rice according to package directions.

4. Divide cauliflower rice among four bowls. Add turkey, cabbage, avocado, tomatoes and green onions. Top with cilantro, sour cream and cotija cheese, if desired.

TIP

For a vegetarian taco bowl, try one of the new plant-based ground meat substitutes on the market—they can be swapped one for one with ground turkey or beef and provide a meaty texture in tacos, chilies, sauces and all your favorite recipes.

CHICKEN FRIED RICE

MAKES 4 SERVINGS

2 tablespoons vegetable oil, divided

12 ounces boneless skinless chicken breasts, cut into ½-inch cubes

Salt and black pepper

2 tablespoons butter

2 cloves garlic, minced

½ sweet onion, diced

1 medium carrot, diced

2 green onions, thinly sliced

3 eggs

4 cups cooked rice*

3 tablespoons soy sauce

2 tablespoons sesame seeds

For rice, cook 1½ cups rice according to package directions without oil or butter. Spread hot rice on large rimmed baking sheet; cool to room temperature. Refrigerate several hours or overnight. Measure 4 cups.

1. Heat 1 tablespoon oil in large skillet over medium-high heat. Add chicken; season with salt and pepper. Cook and stir 5 to 6 minutes or until cooked through. Add butter and garlic; cook and stir 1 minute or until butter is melted. Remove to small bowl.

2. Add sweet onion, carrot and green onions to skillet; cook and stir over high heat 3 minutes or until vegetables are softened. Add to bowl with chicken.

3. Heat remaining 1 tablespoon oil in same skillet. Crack eggs into skillet; cook and stir 45 seconds or until eggs are scrambled but still moist. Add chicken and vegetable mixture, rice, soy sauce and sesame seeds; cook and stir 2 minutes or until well blended and heated through. Season with additional salt and pepper.

TIP

To make a meatless fried rice, substitute 1 package (14 ounces) firm tofu, cut into cubes, for the chicken; brown in oil as directed in step 1. Or, add an additional 1 to 2 cups chopped vegetables (such as bell pepper, green beans, sugar snap peas, snow peas or napa cabbage in step 1; stir-fry in oil until crisp-tender.

ROASTED CHICKPEA AND SWEET POTATO BOWL

MAKES 2 SERVINGS

- 1 **sweet potato (about 12 ounces)**
- 1 **tablespoon plus 1 teaspoon olive oil, divided**
- 1 **teaspoon salt, divided**
- **Black pepper**
- 1 **can (about 15 ounces) chickpeas, rinsed and drained**
- 1 **tablespoon maple syrup**
- 1 **teaspoon paprika, sweet or smoked**
- ½ **teaspoon ground cumin**
- ½ **cup uncooked quinoa, rinsed**
- 1 **cup water**
- **Chopped fresh parsley or cilantro**

TAHINI SAUCE

- ¼ **cup tahini**
- 2 **tablespoons lemon juice**
- 2 **tablespoons water**
- 1 **clove garlic, minced**
- ⅛ **teaspoon salt**

1. Preheat oven to 350°F.

2. Peel sweet potato; cut in half crosswise. Spiral sweet potato with thin ribbon blade of spiralizer. (See Tip.) Cut into 3-inch pieces. Place in 13×9-inch pan. Drizzle with 1 teaspoon oil and sprinkle with ¼ teaspoon salt and black pepper; toss to coat. Push to one side of pan.

3. Combine chickpeas, maple syrup, remaining 1 tablespoon oil, paprika, cumin and ½ teaspoon salt in medium bowl; toss to coat. Spread in other side of pan. Roast 30 minutes, stirring sweet potatoes and chickpeas once or twice..

4. Meanwhile, rinse quinoa under cold water in fine-mesh strainer. Bring 1 cup water, quinoa and ¼ teaspoon salt to a boil in small saucepan. Reduce heat to low; cover and simmer 10 to 15 minutes or until quinoa is tender and water is absorbed.

5. For sauce, whisk tahini, lemon juice, 2 tablespoons water, garlic and ⅛ teaspoon salt in small bowl until smooth. Add additional water if needed to reach desired consistency.

6. Divide quinoa between two bowls. Top with sweet potatoes and chickpeas. Sprinkle with parsley; serve with sauce.

TIP

If you don't have a spiralizer, julienne the sweet potato or cut it into cubes instead.

ROASTED SQUASH WITH TAHINI COUSCOUS

MAKES 4 TO 6 SERVINGS

- 1 butternut squash (about 2½ pounds), peeled and cut into ½-inch cubes
- 2 tablespoons olive oil, divided
- 1¾ teaspoons salt, divided
- 1 package (6 ounces) plain pearled (Israeli) couscous
- 2¾ cups water, divided
- ½ cup tahini
- 1 tablespoon maple syrup
- ¼ teaspoon smoked paprika
- ¼ cup chopped preserved lemon
- Chopped almonds (optional)
- Minced fresh parsley (optional)

1. Preheat oven to 400°F. Combine squash, 1 tablespoon oil and 1 teaspoon salt in medium bowl; toss to coat. Spread in single layer on baking sheet. Roast 30 minutes or until squash is tender and browned, stirring once or twice.

2. Heat remaining 1 tablespoon oil in medium skillet over high heat. Add couscous; cook and stir 2 to 3 minutes or until some of couscous is lightly browned. Stir in ½ teaspoon salt. Add 2½ cups water; bring to a boil. Reduce heat to medium; cook about 10 minutes or until water is mostly absorbed, stirring occasionally. Remove from heat; cover and let stand 5 minutes or until couscous is tender and water is absorbed.

3. Whisk tahini, maple syrup, paprika and remaining ¼ teaspoon salt in small bowl. Whisk in remaining ¼ cup water until smooth. Stir into couscous. Gently stir in squash and preserved lemon; garnish with almonds and parsley. Serve warm.

NOTE

Butternut squash is notoriously difficult to peel. To make the job easier, use a good Y-shaped peeler. Cut a thin slice off the bottom of the squash to give it stability and place it upright on a cutting board. Make downward strokes with the peeler and remove the outer layer of skin. Peel the squash a second time until the bright orange flesh is exposed.

HEARTY VEGGIE SANDWICH

MAKES 4 SERVINGS

- 1 **pound cremini mushrooms, stemmed and thinly sliced (⅛-inch slices)**
- 2 **tablespoons olive oil, divided**
- ¾ **teaspoon salt, divided**
- ¼ **teaspoon black pepper**
- 1 **medium zucchini, diced (¼-inch pieces, about 2 cups)**
- 3 **tablespoons butter, softened**
- 8 **slices artisan whole grain bread**
- ¼ **cup prepared pesto**
- ¼ **cup mayonnaise**
- 2 **cups packed baby spinach**
- 4 **slices (about 1 ounce each) mozzarella cheese**

1. Preheat oven to 350°F. Combine mushrooms, 1 tablespoon oil, ½ teaspoon salt and pepper in medium bowl; toss to coat. Spread in single layer on baking sheet. Roast 20 minutes or until mushrooms are dark brown and dry, stirring after 10 minutes. Cool on baking sheet.

2. Meanwhile, heat remaining 1 tablespoon oil in large skillet over medium heat. Add zucchini and remaining ¼ teaspoon salt; cook and stir 5 minutes or until zucchini is tender and lightly browned. Transfer to bowl; wipe out skillet with paper towels.

3. Spread butter on one side of each bread slice. Turn over slices. Spread pesto on 4 slices; spread mayonnaise on remaining 4 slices. Top pesto-covered slices evenly with mushrooms, then spinach, zucchini and cheese. Top with remaining bread slices, mayonnaise side down.

4. Heat same skillet over medium heat. Add sandwiches; cover and cook 2 minutes per side or until bread is toasted, spinach is slightly wilted and cheese is beginning to melt. Cut sandwiches in half; serve immediately.

GINGER PORK STIR-FRY ON SOBA

MAKES 4 SERVINGS

- 12 ounces pork tenderloin, trimmed
- 2 tablespoons reduced-sodium soy sauce, divided
- 2 teaspoons grated fresh ginger
- 1 clove garlic, minced
- 2 teaspoons coconut oil
- 2 cups fresh sugar snap peas
- 1 small red onion, cut in half and thinly sliced
- 1 teaspoon toasted sesame oil
- ¼ teaspoon hot chili oil or red pepper flakes
- 1 tablespoon minced fresh chives
- 1½ teaspoons minced fresh cilantro
- 2 ounces soba noodles* or whole wheat spaghetti, cooked according to package directions
- 1 small seedless cucumber, cut into thin strips

Soba noodles are Japanese buckwheat noodles that have a dark brown color and a slightly chewy texture.

1. Cut pork into thin strips about 1 inch long.* Place in large bowl. Add 1 tablespoon soy sauce, ginger and garlic; stir to coat. Cover and refrigerate 1 to 2 hours, stirring occasionally.

2. Heat coconut oil in large nonstick skillet over medium-high heat. Add snap peas and onion; cook and stir 5 to 6 minutes or until peas are crisp-tender. Remove to small bowl.

3. Add pork and marinade to same skillet; cook and stir 3 to 5 minutes or until pork is cooked through. Add remaining 1 tablespoon soy sauce, sesame oil and chili oil. Stir in snap peas and onion, chives and cilantro; cook and stir until heated through.

4. Toss soba noodles with cucumber in medium bowl; arrange on four serving plates. Top with pork mixture.

Freeze pork 30 minutes to make slicing easier.

ISLAND FISH TACOS

MAKES 4 SERVINGS

COLESLAW

- **1** medium jicama (about 12 ounces), peeled and shredded
- **2** cups packaged coleslaw mix
- **3** tablespoons finely chopped fresh cilantro
- **¼** cup lime juice
- **¼** cup vegetable oil
- **3** tablespoons white vinegar
- **2** tablespoons mayonnaise
- **1** tablespoon honey
- **1** teaspoon salt

SALSA

- **2** medium fresh tomatoes, diced (about 2 cups)
- **½** cup finely chopped red onion
- **¼** cup finely chopped fresh cilantro
- **2** tablespoons lime juice
- **2** tablespoons minced jalapeño pepper
- **1** teaspoon salt

TACOS

- **1** to 1¼ pounds white fish such as tilapia or mahi mahi, cut into 3×1½-inch pieces
  Salt and black pepper
- **2** tablespoons vegetable oil
- **12** (6-inch) taco-size tortillas, heated
  Prepared guacamole (optional)

1. For coleslaw, combine jicama, coleslaw mix and 3 tablespoons cilantro in medium bowl. Whisk ¼ cup lime juice, ¼ cup oil, vinegar, mayonnaise, honey and 1 teaspoon salt in small bowl until well blended. Pour over vegetable mixture; stir to coat. Let stand at least 15 minutes for flavors to blend.

2. For salsa, place tomatoes in fine-mesh strainer; set in bowl or sink to drain 15 minutes. Transfer to another medium bowl. Stir in onion, ¼ cup cilantro, 2 tablespoons lime juice, jalapeño and 1 teaspoon salt; mix well.

3. For tacos, season both sides of fish with salt and black pepper. Heat 1 tablespoon oil in large nonstick skillet over medium-high heat. Add half of fish; cook about 2 minutes per side or until fish is opaque and begins to flake when tested with fork. Repeat with remaining oil and fish.

4. Serve fish in tortillas with coleslaw and salsa. Serve with guacamole, if desired.

WHOLE WHEAT FLATBREAD WITH HERBED RICOTTA, PEACHES AND ARUGULA

MAKES 4 SERVINGS

½ cup ricotta cheese

2 tablespoons finely chopped fresh basil

½ teaspoon kosher salt

⅛ teaspoon black pepper

2 whole wheat naan breads

1 ripe peach, cut into 12 slices

½ cup arugula

½ teaspoon lemon juice

1 teaspoon extra virgin olive oil

2 teaspoons balsamic vinegar

Flaky sea salt, for sprinkling

1. Preheat oven to 400°F. Line baking sheet with parchment paper.

2. Combine ricotta cheese, basil, kosher salt and pepper in small bowl; mix well. Spread mixture evenly over naan; top with peach slices.

3. Bake 12 minutes or until bottom of naan is crisp.

4. Combine arugula, lemon juice and oil in medium bowl; toss gently. Top baked flatbreads with arugula mixture; drizzle with vinegar and sprinkle with sea salt. Cut each flatbread into quarters.

VEGETABLE SUSHI ROLLS

MAKES 24 PIECES (ABOUT 4 SERVINGS)

- 2 tablespoons unseasoned rice vinegar
- 1 teaspoon sugar
- ½ teaspoon salt
- 2 cups cooked short grain brown rice
- 4 sheets sushi nori
- 1 teaspoon toasted sesame seeds
- ½ English cucumber, cut into thin strips (¼ inch)
- ½ red bell pepper, cut into thin strips (¼ inch)
- ½ ripe avocado, cut into thin pieces (½ inch)
- Pickled ginger and/or wasabi paste (optional)

1. Combine vinegar, sugar and salt in large bowl. Stir in rice. Cover with damp towel until ready to use.

2. Prepare small bowl with water and splash of vinegar to rinse fingers and prevent rice from sticking while working. Place 1 sheet of nori horizontally on bamboo sushi mat or waxed or parchment paper, rough side up. Using wet fingers, spread about ½ cup rice evenly over nori, leaving 1-inch border along bottom edge. Sprinkle rice with ¼ teaspoon sesame seeds. Place one fourth each of cucumber, bell pepper and avocado on top of rice.

3. Pick up edge of mat nearest you. Roll mat forward, wrapping rice around fillings and pressing gently to form log. Press gently to seal. Place roll on cutting board, seam side down. Repeat with remaining nori and fillings.

4. Slice each roll into six pieces using sharp knife.* Cut off ends, if desired. Serve with pickled ginger and/or wasabi, if desired.

Wipe knife with damp cloth between cuts, if necessary.

SESAME GINGER TOFU BAHN MI

MAKES 4 TO 8 SERVINGS

- **4** ounces peeled daikon radish *or* 5 medium red radishes
- **1** large carrot
- **1** tablespoon granulated sugar
- **¾** cup unseasoned rice vinegar
- **1** teaspoon salt
- **1** clove garlic
- **1** piece (1 inch) peeled fresh ginger
- **¼** cup soy sauce
- **1** tablespoon packed brown sugar
- **1** tablespoon dark sesame oil
- **1** package (14 ounces) extra firm tofu, drained, pressed and halved crosswise
- **1** tablespoon grapeseed oil
- **8** ounces seedless cucumber (about 8 inches)
- **1** large loaf (16 ounces) *or* 2 small loaves (8 ounces each) soft French bread, split
- **¼** cup mayonnaise
- Fresh cilantro sprigs
- **1** jalapeño pepper, sliced into rings

1. Spiral radish and carrot with fine spiral blade. (See Tip.) Dissolve granulated sugar in vinegar in 2-cup measuring cup; stir in salt. Measure 1 cup total of carrots and radish; add to vinegar. Let stand at least 1 hour for flavors to blend.

2. Combine garlic and ginger in food processor; process until finely chopped. Add soy sauce, brown sugar and sesame oil; process until smooth. Place tofu in 8-inch square baking dish; pour marinade over tofu. Marinate at room temperature 30 minutes to 1 hour, turning occasionally.

3. Drain tofu, discarding marinade. Heat grapeseed oil in large cast iron skillet over high heat. Working in batches, cook tofu 3 to 4 minutes per side or until well browned. Transfer to paper towel-lined cutting board; let stand until cool enough to handle. Cut into thin slices.

4. Spiral cucumber with large spiral blade. Scoop out some of soft insides of bread. Spread mayonnaise over bottom half of bread; top with tofu, cucumber, carrot mixture, cilantro and jalapeño.

TIP

If you don't have a spiralizer, use a julienne peeler to cut the cucumber, radish and carrot, or cut into julienne strips with a sharp knife.

SPINACH, MUSHROOM, EGG AND GRUYÈRE ROLLUPS

MAKES 4 SERVINGS

- 1 tablespoon plus 4 teaspoons olive oil, divided
- 1 shallot, thinly sliced (about ½ cup)
- 1 package (6 ounces) baby spinach
- 1 clove garlic, minced
- ½ teaspoon plus ⅛ teaspoon salt, divided
- 8 ounces cremini mushrooms, thinly sliced
- ¼ teaspoon black pepper, divided
- 2 pieces flatbread (9½×11 inches), lightly toasted
- ⅔ cup shredded Grùyère cheese
- 6 eggs
- 2 tablespoons milk
- 2 teaspoons Dijon mustard

1. Heat 2 teaspoons oil in large nonstick skillet over medium heat. Add shallot; cook and stir 5 minutes or until softened. Add spinach; cook over medium-high heat 2 minutes or until wilted. Add garlic and ¼ teaspoon salt; cook and stir 1 minute. Remove to small bowl.

2. Heat 1 tablespoon oil in same skillet over medium-high heat. Add mushrooms, ¼ teaspoon salt and ⅛ teaspoon pepper; cook 6 minutes or until browned, stirring occasionally. Stir into spinach mixture.

3. Spread half of spinach-mushroom mixture on each flatbread; top with cheese.

4. Beat eggs in large bowl. Add remaining ⅛ teaspoon salt, ⅛ teaspoon pepper, milk and mustard; beat until blended.

5. Heat remaining 2 teaspoons oil in same skillet over medium-high heat. Add egg mixture; cook about 1 minute or until eggs are set but not dry, stirring frequently.

6. Spread cooked eggs over spinach mixture; roll up flatbread. Cut rolls in half diagonally.

TIP

Roll-ups can be made ahead of time; serve at room temperature or heat in microwave 5 to 10 seconds to warm.

VEGETABLE ENCHILADAS

MAKES 6 SERVINGS

1 tablespoon olive oil

2 large poblano peppers or green bell peppers, thinly sliced

1 large red onion, cut in half and thinly sliced

1 large zucchini, cut into thin strips

1 cup sliced mushrooms

1 teaspoon ground cumin

1 pound fresh tomatillos (about 8 large), peeled

½ to 1 jalapeño pepper,* minced

1 clove garlic

½ teaspoon salt

1 cup loosely packed fresh cilantro

12 corn tortillas, warmed

2 cups (8 ounces) shredded Mexican cheese blend, divided

Jalapeño peppers can sting and irritate the skin, so wear rubber gloves when handling peppers and do not touch your eyes.

1. Preheat oven to 400°F. Spray 13×9-inch baking dish with nonstick cooking spray.

2. Heat oil in large nonstick skillet over medium heat. Add poblano peppers, onion, zucchini, mushrooms and cumin; cook and stir 8 to 10 minutes or until vegetables are crisp-tender.

3. Meanwhile, place tomatillos in large microwavable bowl; cover with vented plastic wrap. Microwave on HIGH 6 to 7 minutes or until very tender.

4. Combine tomatillos with juice, jalapeño, garlic and salt in food processor or blender; process until smooth. Add cilantro; pulse until combined and cilantro is coarsely chopped.

5. Divide vegetables evenly among tortillas. Spoon heaping tablespoon of cheese in center of each tortilla; roll up to enclose filling. Place in prepared baking dish. Pour sauce evenly over enchiladas; sprinkle with remaining 1 cup cheese.

6. Cover and bake 18 to 20 minutes or until cheese is melted and enchiladas are heated through. Serve immediately.

ZUCCHINI AND SWEET POTATO STUFFED PEPPERS

MAKES 4 SERVINGS

- 4 **red bell peppers (about 6 ounces each)**
- 1 **sweet potato, peeled, cut in half, then cut crosswise into ½-inch slices**
- 1 **tablespoon olive oil**
- 1 **medium zucchini, cut into thin strips**
- 1 **small onion, cut in half and thinly sliced**
- ½ **cup diced celery**
- 1 **teaspoon Italian seasoning**
- ¾ **teaspoon salt**
- ¼ **teaspoon black pepper**
- ¼ **cup vegetable broth**
- 2 **tablespoons toasted pine nuts***

*To toast pine nuts, spread on small baking sheet. Bake at 350°F 4 minutes or until lightly browned, stirring frequently.

1. Preheat oven to 375°F. Spray baking dish with nonstick cooking spray.

2. Cut tops off bell peppers; remove seeds and membranes. Bring large pot of water to a boil. Add bell peppers; cover and cook 5 minutes or until peppers begin to soften. Remove from water with tongs; drain upside down on paper towel-lined plate.

3. Place sweet potato in food processor; pulse until finely chopped.

4. Heat oil in large skillet over medium-high heat. Add zucchini, onion, celery, Italian seasoning, salt and black pepper; cook 4 minutes, stirring occasionally. Stir in sweet potatoes; cook 3 minutes or until zucchini is lightly browned.

5. Combine vegetable mixture, broth and pine nuts in large bowl; spoon into bell peppers. Transfer to prepared baking dish. Bake 15 minutes or until sweet potatoes are tender and filling is heated through.

STEAK FAJITAS

MAKES 2 SERVINGS

¼ cup lime juice

¼ cup soy sauce

4 tablespoons vegetable oil, divided

2 tablespoons honey

2 tablespoons Worcestershire sauce

2 cloves garlic, minced

½ teaspoon ground red pepper

1 pound flank steak, skirt steak or top sirloin

1 medium yellow onion, halved and cut into ¼-inch slices

1 green bell pepper, cut into ¼-inch strips

1 red bell pepper, cut into ¼-inch strips

Flour tortillas, warmed

Lime wedges (optional)

Optional toppings: pico de gallo, guacamole, sour cream, shredded lettuce and shredded Cheddar-Jack cheese

1. Combine lime juice, soy sauce, 2 tablespoons oil, honey, Worcestershire sauce, garlic and ground red pepper in medium bowl; mix well. Remove ¼ cup marinade to large bowl. Place steak in large resealable food storage bag. Pour remaining marinade over steak; seal bag and turn to coat. Marinate in refrigerator at least 2 hours or overnight. Add onion and bell peppers to bowl with ¼ cup marinade; toss to coat. Cover and refrigerate until ready to use.

2. Remove steak from marinade; discard marinade and wipe off excess from steak. Heat 1 tablespoon oil in large skillet (preferably cast iron) over medium-high heat. Cook steak about 4 minutes per side for medium rare or to desired doneness. Remove to cutting board; tent with foil and let rest 10 minutes.

3. Meanwhile, heat remaining 1 tablespoon oil in same skillet over medium-high heat. Add vegetable mixture; cook about 8 minutes or until vegetables are crisp-tender and begin to brown in spots, stirring occasionally. (Cook in two batches if necessary; do not crowd vegetables in skillet.)

4. Cut steak into thin slices across the grain. Serve with vegetables, tortillas, lime wedges and desired toppings.

TIP

For vegetable fajitas, simply omit the steak and double the vegetables; cook as directed in step 3. Serve with warm black beans for additional protein.

ZOODLES IN TOMATO SAUCE

MAKES 4 SERVINGS

- **3 teaspoons olive oil, divided**
- **2 cloves garlic**
- **1 tablespoon tomato paste**
- **1 can (28 ounces) whole tomatoes, undrained**
- **1 teaspoon dried oregano**
- **½ teaspoon salt**
- **2 large zucchini (about 16 ounces each), ends trimmed, cut into 3-inch pieces**
- **¼ cup shredded Parmesan cheese**

1. Heat 2 teaspoons oil in medium saucepan over medium heat. Add garlic; cook 1 minute or until fragrant but not browned. Add tomato paste; cook 30 seconds, stirring constantly. Add tomatoes with juice, oregano and salt, breaking up tomatoes with wooden spoon. Bring to a simmer. Reduce heat to medium-low; cook 30 minutes or until sauce is thickened.

2. Meanwhile, spiral zucchini with fine spiral blade. (See Tip.)

3. Heat remaining 1 teaspoon oil in large skillet over medium-high heat. Add zucchini; cook 4 to 5 minutes or until tender, stirring frequently. Transfer to serving plates; top with tomato sauce and cheese.

TIP

If you don't have a spiralizer, cut the zucchini into ribbons with a mandoline or sharp knife. Or purchase zucchini spirals in the produce section of the supermarket.

MEDITERRANEAN GRILLED FLATBREADS

MAKES 4 SERVINGS

⅓ cup extra virgin olive oil

3 tablespoons red wine vinegar

1 clove garlic, minced

1 teaspoon dried oregano

1 teaspoon dried mint

¾ teaspoon salt

½ teaspoon black pepper

¼ teaspoon red pepper flakes

1 pound turkey or chicken breast cutlets

1 small eggplant, cut crosswise into ¼-inch slices

1 large zucchini, cut crosswise into ¼-inch slices

2 medium onions, cut in half vertically

1 red bell pepper, cut into quarters

1 yellow bell pepper, cut into quarters

4 flatbreads or naan breads

Crumbled goat cheese and fresh Italian parsley sprigs

1. Whisk oil, vinegar, garlic, oregano, mint, salt, black pepper and red pepper flakes in large bowl until well blended. Remove half of mixture to shallow dish; add turkey and turn to coat. Let stand 15 minutes.

2. Meanwhile, prepare grill for direct cooking. Oil grid. Brush one side of eggplant and zucchini with oil mixture. Brush cut sides of onions and bell peppers with oil mixture.

3. Place vegetables, seasoned sides down, on grid. Grill over medium-high heat about 10 minutes or until vegetables are browned and tender, turning once and brushing with remaining oil mixture. Remove to plate.

4. Remove turkey from marinade; discard marinade. Grill 4 to 5 minutes per side or until no longer pink in center. Remove to clean plate.

5. Cut onions and bell peppers into strips; cut eggplant and zucchini slices into halves or quarters. Combine vegetables on serving platter.

6. Grill flatbreads, covered, 1 to 3 minutes or until lightly browned. Serve flatbreads with vegetables and turkey; top with cheese and parsley.

TIP
Use a grill basket to make grilling vegetables easier—you can turn all the vegetables at once and there's no worry about pieces falling through the grates.

ROASTED CHICKEN WITH CABBAGE

MAKES 4 SERVINGS

⅓ cup olive oil, plus additional for pan

2 tablespoons red wine vinegar

2 cloves garlic, minced

1 teaspoon salt

1 teaspoon onion powder

¼ teaspoon paprika

¼ teaspoon black pepper

8 bone-in, skin-on chicken thighs (about 3 pounds)

2 large onions, cut into ½-inch slices (do not separate into rings)

1 small head green cabbage (about 2 pounds)

Chopped fresh parsley (optional)

1. Preheat oven to 425°F. Brush baking sheet with oil.

2. Whisk ⅓ cup oil, vinegar, garlic, salt, onion powder, paprika and pepper in large bowl until well blended. Remove half of mixture to medium bowl; add chicken and turn to coat.

3. Add onion slices to large bowl with oil mixture; turn to coat. Arrange in single layer on prepared baking sheet. Cut cabbage in half through core (do not remove core). Cut each half into 1-inch wedges. Add cabbage to bowl with oil mixture; turn to coat. Arrange cabbage over onions on baking sheet. Place chicken, skin side up, on top of cabbage.

4. Roast 50 to 55 minutes or until chicken is 165°F. Remove chicken to plate; tent with foil to keep warm. Carefully drain liquid from baking sheet. Stir vegetables; roast 10 to 15 minutes or until edges begin to brown and cabbage is crisp-tender. Serve chicken with vegetables. Garnish with parsley.

VEGETABLES & SIDES

WHOLE ROASTED CAULIFLOWER

MAKES 4 TO 6 SERVINGS

6 tablespoons olive oil, divided

1 head cauliflower, leaves trimmed

½ teaspoon plus ⅛ teaspoon salt, divided

Black pepper

¼ cup water

¾ cup panko bread crumbs

¼ cup shredded Parmesan cheese

1 clove garlic, minced

¼ teaspoon dried oregano

¼ teaspoon dried sage

⅛ teaspoon red pepper flakes

1. Preheat oven to 400°F. Line 13×9-inch baking pan with foil.

2. Rub 4 tablespoons oil all over cauliflower, 1 tablespoon at at time. Sprinkle with ½ teaspoon salt and black pepper. Place cauliflower in prepared pan; pour water into bottom pan. Roast 45 minutes, adding additional water if pan is dry.

3. Combine panko, cheese, garlic, oregano, sage, red pepper flakes and remaining ⅛ teaspoon salt in small bowl. Stir in remaining 2 tablespoons oil.

4. Remove pan from oven; carefully pat panko mixture all over and under cauliflower. Bake 15 minutes or until panko is browned and cauliflower is tender. Cut into wedges to serve.

SERVING SUGGESTION

Serve with a simple kale salad. Combine 6 cups shredded kale, 1 clove minced garlic and 2 tablespoons olive oil in a large bowl; season with salt and black pepper. Mix with hands, rubbing oil into kale until kale is glossy and softened slightly.

BALSAMIC BUTTERNUT SQUASH

MAKES 4 SERVINGS

3 tablespoons olive oil

2 tablespoons thinly sliced fresh sage (about 6 large leaves), divided

1 medium butternut squash, peeled and cut into 1-inch pieces (4 to 5 cups)

½ red onion, cut in half and cut into ¼-inch slices

1 teaspoon salt, divided

2½ tablespoons balsamic vinegar

¼ teaspoon black pepper

1. Heat oil in large cast iron skillet over medium-high heat. Add 1 tablespoon sage; cook and stir 3 minutes. Add squash, onion and ½ teaspoon salt; cook 6 minutes, stirring occasionally. Reduce heat to medium; cook 15 minutes without stirring.

2. Stir in vinegar, remaining ½ teaspoon salt and pepper; cook 10 minutes or until squash is tender, stirring occasionally. Stir in remaining 1 tablespoon sage; cook 1 minute.

MEDITERRANEAN ORZO AND VEGETABLE PILAF

MAKES 6 SERVINGS

4 ounces (½ cup plus 2 tablespoons) uncooked orzo pasta

1 tablespoon olive oil

1 small onion, diced

2 cloves garlic, minced

1 small zucchini, diced

½ cup chicken broth

1 can (about 14 ounces) artichoke hearts, drained and quartered

1 medium tomato, chopped

½ teaspoon dried oregano

½ teaspoon salt

¼ teaspoon black pepper

½ cup crumbled feta cheese

Sliced black olives (optional)

1. Cook orzo according to package directions; drain and set aside.

2. Heat oil in large nonstick skillet over medium heat. Add onion; cook and stir 5 minutes or until translucent. Add garlic; cook and stir 1 minute. Add zucchini and broth; cook over low heat 5 minutes or until zucchini is crisp-tender.

3. Add cooked orzo, artichokes, tomato, oregano, salt and pepper to skillet; cook and stir 1 minute or until heated through. Top with cheese and olives, if desired.

ROASTED ASPARAGUS WITH SHALLOT VINAIGRETTE

MAKES 4 SERVINGS

1 **pound fresh asparagus**

4 **tablespoons olive oil, divided**

1 **shallot, minced**

1 **tablespoon balsamic or white wine vinegar**

¼ **teaspoon salt**

¼ **teaspoon black pepper**

1. Preheat oven to 425°F. Spread asparagus in shallow baking pan or on baking sheet. Drizzle with 1 tablespoon oil; toss to coat.

2. Roast asparagus 10 minutes or until tender and lightly browned. Transfer to serving plate.

3. Meanwhile, whisk remaining 3 tablespoons oil, shallot, vinegar, salt and pepper in small bowl until well blended. Let stand at least 5 minutes to allow flavors to blend. Spoon vinaigrette over asparagus.

BARLEY AND VEGETABLE RISOTTO

MAKES 4 TO 6 SERVINGS

4½ cups vegetable or chicken broth

1 tablespoon olive oil

1 small onion, chopped

8 ounces sliced mushrooms

¾ cup uncooked pearl barley

1 large red bell pepper, diced

2 cups packed baby spinach

¼ cup grated Parmesan cheese

¼ teaspoon black pepper

1. Bring broth to a boil in medium saucepan. Reduce heat to low to keep broth hot.

2. Meanwhile, heat oil in large saucepan over medium-high heat. Add onion; cook and stir 3 minutes. Add mushrooms; cook 5 minutes or until mushrooms begin to brown and liquid evaporates, stirring frequently.

3. Add barley; cook 1 minute. Add broth, ¼ cup at a time, stirring constantly until broth is almost absorbed before adding the next ¼ cup.

4. After 20 minutes of cooking, stir in bell pepper. Continue adding broth, ¼ cup at a time, until barley is tender (about 30 minutes total). Stir in spinach; cook 1 minute or just until spinach is wilted. Stir in cheese and black pepper.

TIP

Use your favorite mushrooms, such as button, crimini or shiitake, or a combination of two or more.

SWEET POTATO NOODLES WITH BLUE CHEESE AND WALNUTS

MAKES 2 SERVINGS

- 2 sweet potatoes (1½ pounds)
- ¼ cup chopped walnuts
- 1 tablespoon olive oil
- 2 cloves garlic, minced
- ¼ cup whipping cream
- 1 package (about 5 ounces) baby spinach
- ¼ cup crumbled blue cheese
- ¼ teaspoon salt
- ¼ teaspoon black pepper

1. Spiral sweet potatoes with thin ribbon blade. Loosely pile on cutting board; cut pile horizontally and vertically with sharp knife to make shorter pieces.

2. Cook walnuts in large nonstick skillet over medium-high heat 3 to 4 minutes or until toasted, stirring frequently. Remove to plate; cool completely.

3. Heat oil in same skillet over medium-high heat. Add sweet potatoes; cook 10 minutes or until potatoes reach desired doneness, stirring occasionally and adding water by tablespoonfuls if sweet potatoes are browning too quickly.

4. Add garlic to skillet; cook and stir 30 seconds. Add cream and spinach; cook and stir 1 minute or until cream is absorbed and spinach is wilted. Transfer to bowls; top with walnuts and cheese. Season with salt and pepper.

PUMPKIN POLENTA

MAKES 4 SERVINGS

- 1 **tablespoon olive oil**
- 1 **tablespoon butter, plus additional for serving**
- 1 **medium onion, chopped**
- ½ **teaspoon smoked paprika**
- ½ **teaspoon salt**
- ¼ **teaspoon ground mace or nutmeg**
- ⅛ **teaspoon ground red pepper**
- 1 **can (15 ounces) pure pumpkin**
- 2 **cups vegetable broth or water**
- 1 **cup milk**
- 1 **cup instant polenta**
- ½ **cup (2 ounces) shredded fontina cheese, plus additional for serving**
- **Fresh thyme sprigs (optional)**

1. Heat oil and 1 tablespoon butter in medium saucepan over medium heat. Add onion; cook and stir 5 minutes or until softened. Add paprika, salt, mace and red pepper; cook 30 seconds, stirring constantly. Add pumpkin; cook 2 minutes, stirring frequently.

2. Whisk in broth and milk; bring to a boil over high heat. Stir in polenta in thin, steady stream. Reduce heat to medium-high; cook 5 minutes or until very thick, stirring constantly.

3. Remove from heat; stir in ½ cup cheese until melted. Top each serving with additional butter and cheese, if desired. Garnish with fresh thyme.

ROASTED CURRIED CAULIFLOWER AND BRUSSELS SPROUTS

MAKES 10 SERVINGS

2 pounds cauliflower florets

12 ounces brussels sprouts, trimmed and cut in half lengthwise

⅓ cup olive oil

2½ tablespoons curry powder

½ teaspoon sea salt

½ teaspoon black pepper

½ cup chopped fresh cilantro

1. Preheat oven to 400°F. Line large baking sheet with foil.

2. Combine cauliflower, brussels sprouts and oil in large bowl; toss to coat. Sprinkle with curry powder, salt and pepper; toss to coat. Spread vegetables in single layer on prepared baking sheet.

3. Roast 20 to 25 minutes or until golden brown, stirring after 15 minutes. Add cilantro; toss until blended.

RED CABBAGE WITH BACON AND MUSHROOMS

MAKES ABOUT 6 SERVINGS

- 4 slices thick-cut bacon, chopped
- 1 onion, chopped
- 1 package (8 ounces) cremini mushrooms, chopped (½-inch pieces)
- ¾ teaspoon dried thyme
- ½ medium red cabbage, cut into wedges, cored and then cut crosswise into ¼-inch slices (about 7 cups)
- ¾ teaspoon salt
- ¼ teaspoon black pepper
- ⅔ cup chicken broth
- 3 tablespoons cider vinegar
- ¼ cup chopped walnuts, toasted*
- 3 tablespoons chopped fresh parsley

*To toast walnuts, cook in small skillet over medium heat 3 to 4 minutes or until lightly browned, stirring frequently.

1. Cook bacon in large saucepan or skillet over medium-high heat until crisp. Remove to paper towel-lined plate.

2. Add onion to saucepan; cook and stir 5 minutes or until softened. Add mushrooms and thyme; cook about 6 minutes or until mushrooms begin to brown, stirring occasionally. Add cabbage, ¾ teaspoon salt and ¼ teaspoon pepper; cook about 7 minutes or until cabbage has wilted.

3. Stir in broth, vinegar and half of bacon; bring to a boil. Reduce heat to low; cook, uncovered, 15 to 20 minutes or until cabbage is tender.

4. Stir in walnuts and parsley; season with additional salt and pepper if necessary. Sprinkle with remaining bacon.

TIP

Make it meatless by omitting the bacon and cooking the vegetables in 1 tablespoon olive oil in step 2. Increase the salt to 1 teaspoon and add ¼ teaspoon smoked paprika.

GARLIC PARMESAN SPAGHETTI SQUASH

MAKES 2 SERVINGS

- **3** tablespoons olive oil, divided
- **1** medium spaghetti squash (2 to 2½ pounds)
- **¼** teaspoon plus ⅛ teaspoon salt, divided
- **1** clove garlic, minced
- **¼** teaspoon red pepper flakes
- **⅛** teaspoon black pepper
- **½** cup shredded Parmesan cheese
- **⅓** cup chopped fresh parsley

1. Preheat oven to 400°F. Brush baking sheet with 1 teaspoon oil. Cut squash in half; remove and discard seeds. Brush each cut side with 1 teaspoon oil; sprinkle with ⅛ teaspoon salt. Place squash halves cut sides down on prepared baking sheet.

2. Bake 30 to 40 minutes or until squash is fork-tender.

3. Remove squash to plate; let stand until cool enough to handle. Use fork to shred squash into long strands, reserving shells for serving, if desired.

4. Heat remaining 2 tablespoons oil in large nonstick skillet over medium-high heat. Add garlic, remaining ¼ teaspoon salt, red pepper flakes and black pepper; cook and stir 2 to 3 minutes or until garlic begins to turn golden. Add squash, cheese and parsley to skillet; cook and stir gently over medium heat just until blended. Serve immediately.

SKILLET ROASTED ROOT VEGETABLES

MAKES 4 SERVINGS

1 **sweet potato, peeled, cut in half lengthwise and cut crosswise into ½-inch slices**

1 **large red onion, cut into 1-inch wedges**

2 **parsnips, cut diagonally into 1-inch slices**

2 **carrots, cut diagonally into 1-inch slices**

1 **turnip, peeled, cut in half and then cut into ½-inch slices**

2½ **tablespoons olive oil**

1½ **tablespoons honey**

1½ **tablespoons balsamic vinegar**

1 **teaspoon kosher salt**

1 **teaspoon dried thyme**

¼ **teaspoon ground red pepper**

¼ **teaspoon black pepper**

1. Preheat oven to 400°F.

2. Combine all ingredients in large bowl; toss to coat. Spread vegetables in single layer in large cast iron skillet.

3. Roast 1 hour or until vegetables are tender, stirring once halfway through cooking time.

FARRO RISOTTO WITH MUSHROOMS AND SPINACH

MAKES 4 SERVINGS

2 tablespoons olive oil

1 medium onion, chopped

12 ounces cremini mushrooms, stems trimmed and quartered

¾ teaspoon salt

¼ teaspoon black pepper

2 cloves garlic, minced

1 cup uncooked farro

1 sprig fresh thyme

4 cups vegetable broth

1 package (about 5 ounces) baby spinach

¼ cup grated Parmesan cheese

1. Heat oil in large skillet or saucepan over medium heat. Add onion, mushrooms, salt and pepper; cook 8 minutes or until tender, stirring occasionally. Add garlic; cook and stir 1 minute. Stir in farro and thyme; cook 1 minute.

2. Stir in broth; bring to a boil. Reduce heat to low; cover and simmer 25 to 30 minutes or until farro is tender and broth is absorbed, stirring occasionally.

3. Remove and discard thyme sprig. Stir in spinach and cheese just before serving.

CORNMEAL-CRUSTED CAULIFLOWER STEAKS

MAKES 4 SERVINGS

½ cup cornmeal

¼ cup all-purpose flour

1 teaspoon salt

1 teaspoon dried sage

½ teaspoon garlic powder

Black pepper

½ cup milk

2 heads cauliflower

¼ cup (½ stick) butter, melted

1. Preheat oven to 400°F. Line baking sheet with parchment paper.

2. Combine cornmeal, flour, salt, sage and garlic powder in shallow bowl or baking pan. Season with pepper. Pour milk into another shallow bowl.

3. Turn cauliflower stem side up on cutting board. Trim away leaves, leaving stem intact. Slice through stem into 3 slices. Trim off excess florets from end slices, creating flat "steaks." Repeat with remaining cauliflower. Reserve extra cauliflower for another use.

4. Dip cauliflower slices into milk to coat both sides. Place in cornmeal mixture; pat onto all sides of cauliflower. Place on prepared baking sheet; drizzle with butter.

5. Bake 40 minutes or until cauliflower is tender.

ORZO WITH SPINACH AND RED PEPPER

MAKES 4 SERVINGS

4 ounces uncooked orzo pasta

1 tablespoon olive oil

1 medium red bell pepper, diced

3 cloves garlic, minced

1 package (10 ounces) frozen chopped spinach, thawed and squeezed dry

¼ cup grated Parmesan cheese

½ teaspoon salt

½ teaspoon finely chopped fresh oregano or basil

¼ teaspoon lemon-pepper seasoning

1. Prepare orzo according to package directions; drain and set aside.

2. Heat oil in large nonstick skillet over medium-high heat. Add bell pepper and garlic; cook and stir 2 to 3 minutes or until bell pepper is crisp-tender. Add orzo and spinach; cook and stir until heated through.

3. Remove from heat; stir in cheese, salt, oregano and lemon-pepper seasoning. Serve immediately.

METRIC CONVERSION CHART

VOLUME MEASUREMENTS (dry)

$1/8$ teaspoon = 0.5 mL
$1/4$ teaspoon = 1 mL
$1/2$ teaspoon = 2 mL
$3/4$ teaspoon = 4 mL
1 teaspoon = 5 mL
1 tablespoon = 15 mL
2 tablespoons = 30 mL
$1/4$ cup = 60 mL
$1/3$ cup = 75 mL
$1/2$ cup = 125 mL
$2/3$ cup = 150 mL
$3/4$ cup = 175 mL
1 cup = 250 mL
2 cups = 1 pint = 500 mL
3 cups = 750 mL
4 cups = 1 quart = 1 L

VOLUME MEASUREMENTS (fluid)

1 fluid ounce (2 tablespoons) = 30 mL
4 fluid ounces ($1/2$ cup) = 125 mL
8 fluid ounces (1 cup) = 250 mL
12 fluid ounces ($1 1/2$ cups) = 375 mL
16 fluid ounces (2 cups) = 500 mL

WEIGHTS (mass)

$1/2$ ounce = 15 g
1 ounce = 30 g
3 ounces = 90 g
4 ounces = 120 g
8 ounces = 225 g
10 ounces = 285 g
12 ounces = 360 g
16 ounces = 1 pound = 450 g

DIMENSIONS

$1/16$ inch = 2 mm
$1/8$ inch = 3 mm
$1/4$ inch = 6 mm
$1/2$ inch = 1.5 cm
$3/4$ inch = 2 cm
1 inch = 2.5 cm

OVEN TEMPERATURES

250°F = 120°C
275°F = 140°C
300°F = 150°C
325°F = 160°C
350°F = 180°C
375°F = 190°C
400°F = 200°C
425°F = 220°C
450°F = 230°C

BAKING PAN SIZES

Utensil	Size in Inches/Quarts	Metric Volume	Size in Centimeters
Baking or Cake Pan (square or rectangular)	$8 \times 8 \times 2$	2 L	$20 \times 20 \times 5$
	$9 \times 9 \times 2$	2.5 L	$23 \times 23 \times 5$
	$12 \times 8 \times 2$	3 L	$30 \times 20 \times 5$
	$13 \times 9 \times 2$	3.5 L	$33 \times 23 \times 5$
Loaf Pan	$8 \times 4 \times 3$	1.5 L	$20 \times 10 \times 7$
	$9 \times 5 \times 3$	2 L	$23 \times 13 \times 7$
Round Layer Cake Pan	$8 \times 1 1/2$	1.2 L	20×4
	$9 \times 1 1/2$	1.5 L	23×4
Pie Plate	$8 \times 1 1/4$	750 mL	20×3
	$9 \times 1 1/4$	1 L	23×3
Baking Dish or Casserole	1 quart	1 L	—
	$1 1/2$ quart	1.5 L	—
	2 quart	2 L	—